Remembering Hedley

Remembering Hedley

Edited by Coral Bell and Meredith Thatcher

ANU

THE AUSTRALIAN NATIONAL UNIVERSITY

E PRESS

ANU
E PRESS

Published by ANU E Press
The Australian National University
Canberra ACT 0200, Australia
Email: anuepress@anu.edu.au
This title is also available online at: http://epress.anu.edu.au/hedley_citation.html

National Library of Australia
Cataloguing-in-Publication entry

Title:	Remembering Hedley / editors, Meredith Thatcher ; Coral Bell.
ISBN:	9781921536069 (pbk.) 9781921536076 (pdf)
Series:	Working paper (Australian National University. Strategic and Defence Studies Centre) ; no. 170.
Subjects:	National security. International relations. Festschriften. Essays.
Other Authors/Contributors:	Thatcher, Meredith. Bell, Coral
Dewey Number:	355.03

The *Canberra Papers on Strategy and Defence* series is a collection of publications arising principally from research undertaken at the SDSC. Canberra Papers have been peer reviewed since 2006. All Canberra Papers are available for sale: visit the SDSC website at <http://rspas. anu.edu.au/sdsc/canberra_papers.php> for abstracts and prices. Electronic copies (in pdf format) of most SDSC Working Papers published since 2002 may be downloaded for free from the SDSC website at <http://rspas.anu.edu.au/sdsc/working_papers.php>. The entire Working Papers series is also available on a 'print on demand' basis.

Cover design by ANU E Press

Contents

Contributors

Robert Ayson is Senior Fellow in The Australian National University's Strategic and Defence Studies Centre where he directs the Graduate Studies in Strategy and Defence Program. He has held official positions in New Zealand with the External Assessments Bureau and the Foreign Affairs, Defence and Trade parliamentary select committee, and academic positions at the University of Waikato and Massey University. Dr Ayson is the author of *Thomas Schelling and the Nuclear Age: Strategy as Social Science*, published by Frank Cass in 2004, and co-editor (with Desmond Ball) of *Strategy and Security in the Asia-Pacific*, published by Allen & Unwin in 2006. His research interests include strategic concepts, Asia-Pacific security, Australasian strategic policies and nuclear proliferation issues.

Coral Bell is a Visiting Fellow at the Strategic and Defence Studies Centre, The Australian National University. She has held postings in the Diplomatic Service and as Professor of International Politics at the University of Sussex. Her research interests are mainly in crisis management and the interaction of strategic, economic and diplomatic factors in international politics, especially as they affect US and Australian foreign policies. Her articles have appeared in a number of leading international journals, such as *Foreign Affairs*, *The National Interest* and *The American Interest*. Recent publications have included *Living with Giants: Finding Australia's place in a more complex world* and *A World Out of Balance: American Power and International Politics in the Twenty-First Century*. She also contributed 'The International System and Changing Strategic Norms' in (eds) R. Ayson and D. Ball, *Strategy and Security in the Asia-Pacific* and authored *The End of the Vasco da Gama Era: The next landscape of world politics*, published by the Lowy Institute for International Policy and Longueville Media in December 2007.

Mary Bull was married to Hedley Bull soon after both graduated from the University of Sydney. Her scholarly interests have been in the field of African studies, and she worked for a time with Professor Marjorie Perham, as well as raising three children.

Professor Sir Michael Howard OM, is a British military historian, former Chichele Professor of the History of War and Regius Professor of Modern History at Oxford University, and Robert A. Lovett Professor of Military and Naval History at Yale University. Howard served during the Second World War, was twice wounded and won a Military Cross at Salerno. He helped found the Department of War Studies and the Liddell Hart Centre for Military Archives at King's College, London, as well as the International Institute for Strategic Studies. He was knighted in 1986 and was appointed to the Order of the Companions of Honour in 2002 and to the Order of Merit in 2005. He is an authority on Carl von Clausewitz, including as co-editor and translator (with Peter Paret) of *Carl von Clausewitz, On War* and as author of *Clausewitz*. Other publications include *Disengagement in Europe*; *Studies in War and Peace*; *The Continental Commitment: The Dilemma of British Defence Policy in the Era of Two World Wars*; *War in European History*; *Soldiers and Governments: Nine Studies in Civil Military Relations*; *Strategic Deception in World War II*; *The Lessons of History*; *The Invention of Peace*; *The First World War*; and, in 2007, *Liberation or Catastrophe?: Reflections on the History of the 20th Century*. His autobiography, entitled *Captain Professor: A Life in War and Peace*, was published by Continuum International Publishing Group in 2006.

Renée Jeffrey joined the School of History and Politics at the University of Adelaide as a Lecturer in International Politics in July 2007. She was previously a lecturer in International Relations in the Politics Program at La Trobe University. Jeffery was awarded her BA(Hons) from the University of New South Wales and her PhD in International Relations from the University of St. Andrews. Her research interests include international ethics, international relations theory, international law, the history of international thought, and religion and international politics. Jeffery's publications include *Hugo Grotius in International Thought* and *Evil and International Relations: Human Suffering in an Age of Terror*. Jeffery is also the editor of *Confronting Evil in International Relations: Ethical Responses to Problems of Moral Agency*, which was published by Palgrave Macmillan in May 2008.

Bruce Miller, an Emeritus Professor of The Australian National University, was its Professor of International Relations from 1962 to 1987 and before that Professor of Politics at Leicester University in the United Kingdom. He had a distinguished career both in academia and in Australian public life, serving on, amongst other organisations, the Australian Research Grants Committee, the Australian Commission for UNESCO (twice) and the Australian Population and Immigration Council. His intellectual interests ranged widely, with its core, at least in publication, centering on Australia in the Commonwealth and in the wider world. His more than a dozen books included *The Politics of the Third World*; *Survey of Commonwealth Affairs: Problems of Expansion and Attrition*; *The EEC and Australia*; *The World of States*; *Ideology and Foreign Policy*; and two highly regarded textbooks for students of political science, *Australian Government and Politics*, and *The Nature of Politics*.

Robert O'Neill is currently Planning Director of the United States Studies Centre of the University of Sydney. He has been director of the International Institute for Strategic Studies in London, Chichele Professor of the History of War at the University of Oxford, a Fellow of All Souls College and Chairman of the Sir Robert Menzies Centre for Australian Studies in the University of London (1990–96). He is also a board member of the Lowy Institute for International

Policy. His research interests focus on war and warfare in the past and present, and ways of resolving international tensions. While Head of the Strategic and Defence Studies Centre at the Australian National University (1970–82), he wrote the *Official History of Australia's role in the Korean War* and he is also the former Armed Services Editor of the *Australian Dictionary of Biography* (1970–2001). He was elected a Fellow of the Academy of the Social Sciences in Australia in 1978 and awarded an Order of Australia in 1988.

Adam Watson was an international relations theorist and researcher. Alongside Hedley Bull, Martin Wight, Herbert Butterfield, and others, he was one of the founding members of the English school of international relations theory. He joined the British Diplomatic Service in 1937. After retiring early, he entered academia, first at The Australian National University, at the invitation of Hedley Bull, and then in the United States, where he was Professor of International Studies at the University of Virginia. In the late 1950s, he was instrumental in facilitating the funding of the British Committee on the Theory of International Politics and became a member, attending when he was in the United Kingdom, and later becoming its third chairman, in succession to Butterfield and Wight. He was instrumental in the production (co-edited with Hedley Bull) of *The Expansion of International Society*, a key international relations text. He wrote numerous other publications, including *The Nature and Problems of the Third World*; *The Evolution of International Society: A Comparative Historical Analysis*; *The Limits of Independence*; *International Relations and the Practice of Hegemony*; and *Diplomacy: the Dialogue between States*. Adam Watson died on 24 August 2007, the same year that Routledge published his final volume, *Hegemony & History*.

Foreword

When Hedley Bull was a young man, his intellectual influence was more visible in the 'corridors of power' in London than in his native Australia. Because his first book, on control of the arms race, was so powerfully argued and convincing, he was appointed (when Harold Wilson was UK Prime Minister) to head the arms control research unit at the British Foreign Office in the middle years of the Cold War, when the strategies were being implemented which led to its ultimately peaceful outcome. Professor Robert J. O'Neill has written an authoritative analysis of his arms-control doctrine for this book.

Hedley was an influential voice also in the formative early years (about the same time) of the now worldwide International Institute for Strategic Studies (IISS), as Michael Howard's brilliant and touching memorial tribute testifies. So, as an analysis of foreign policy and strategy, he was concerned primarily with the world picture, and it thus seems appropriate that his name should be commemorated in a building whose future scholars and students will be much preoccupied with that picture. Especially as Hedley (as Michael also testifies) always remained firmly, even defiantly, Australian.

In later years, indeed, he became particularly absorbed in an issue of primary importance to Australia—the future of Asia, especially China and India. While he was at The Australian National University, he was a member of a group which travelled in China in 1973, while Mao Zedong was still alive, and the country was still in the throes of the 'Great Proletarian Cultural Revolution'—a very different place to its present self. In India he cultivated connections at Jawaharlal Nehru University. The volume that he edited with Adam Watson, *The Expansion of International Society*, was a major testimony to that new focus, and if Hedley had lived longer he was intending further research in the area, especially on the revolt of the non-Western world against the West. Since the best way of knowing a writer is to read his work, I have included in this book three of Hedley's less easily available essays.

Hedley and I were both members also of a little-known, but in some ways influential, small group—the British Committee on International Theory, of which I give a brief account in this book. For both of us the central interest of its work was that Martin Wight, a notable scholar who was at the London School of Economics (LSE) in the years that each of us spent there, and who was a vivid influence on us both, wrote regular essays for its meetings. Martin was an old-fashioned academic who liked to spend most of his energy on students rather than on securing publication, and most of his books have been published posthumously through the efforts of devoted friends and students. Hedley was prominent in that endeavour, so the degree to which Martin's thought is now more widely known owes much to him.

In his Canberra years, as a professor at The Australian National University, Hedley was busy mostly writing his best-known and most influential book, *The Anarchical Society: A Study of Order in World Politics*, which was published soon after he had returned to Oxford. An account of his years in Canberra has been written by his close friend and colleague, Professor Bruce Miller. Hedley was not only a brilliant and creative analyst, but a devoted and charismatic teacher. And in many ways he always seemed to remain essentially (as I was myself) a product of Sydney University in John Anderson's time. Dr Renée Jeffery has provided a cogent analysis of that influence. Dr Robert Ayson has written an illuminating account of the convergence and conflicts between Hedley's intellect and another formidable mind, Professor Thomas Schelling.

My thanks are due to all of them, but most especially to Mary Bull, Hedley's life-long partner from their student days at Sydney onwards, and a scholar in her own right. Since the basic idea of this book is that people should present their spontaneous recollections of Hedley, or their reactions to his work, no editorial effort has been made to eliminate the inevitable overlappings. Any errors that remain are my responsibility.

Coral Bell
July 2008

Chapter 1

Early Years: Sydney and Oxford

Mary Bull

Hedley Bull entered Sydney University in March 1949, at the age of 16, to study for an Arts/Law degree. He did not come from an academic background; his father, Norman Bull, worked in insurance, and his mother was born Doris Hordern of the Sydney department store dynasty. However, his elder brother and sister had both obtained degrees at Sydney, and law seemed the most appropriate career for Hedley, who never liked mathematics or science, but had done well in languages and school debating. Living in the suburb of Strathfield, he had been able to attend Fort Street High School, one of the most prestigious state schools in the New South Wales' system of selective high schools. However, he had not had an outstanding school career, for it was only in the last six months, he later said, that he decided that he wished to proceed to university and settled down to work. Nor had he been a sportsman; he was never interested in playing or watching team games, but preferred non-competitive exercise, primarily swimming, surfing, tennis and walking.

Students of the Arts/Law degree chose subjects in the Arts Faculty for their first year—Hedley took English, history, philosophy and psychology. When in the second year law subjects became the major part of the syllabus, Hedley decided that he preferred to continue studying for an Arts degree—and changed course to read for an Honours degree in philosophy and history. He never lost his interest in law, particularly in the influence of legal theorists in the development of political and international thought, and their concepts of natural law and justice. But for the next three years, Hedley's main interest was in philosophy, in which he was deeply influenced by the ideas of his professor, John Anderson.

Much has been written on Anderson's philosophical teaching, and of his influence on his students. He had been appointed from Glasgow to the Challis Chair of Philosophy at Sydney in 1927 and immediately shocked the staid citizens of Sydney by advocating atheism and communism. Demands for his removal ended in a compromise; the philosophy department was divided into two, and students had a choice of studying logic and metaphysics under Anderson, or moral and political philosophy under another Scot, Professor A.K. Stout. However, this did not prevent Anderson speaking outside the lecture room on these subjects. His support of communism did not last, and the Moscow trials of the 1930s disillusioned him completely, so by 1950 he was supporting the freedom of all political views to be heard. Hedley chose Anderson's course, regarded as the tough option, and thus received a thorough grounding in the Greek and Western European classics of philosophy. But it meant that he did not then study political or moral theorists, even though, as Bruce Miller recalls, he attempted at this time to form a Political Science Association. He associated with other 'Andersonians' in the Free Thought Society, which was believed by other students to advocate free love as well as free thought, and which certainly attacked all conventional beliefs. Hedley learnt two major doctrines from Anderson which influenced him for the rest of his life. The first was that the academic life—a life to which he was increasingly attracted—should be a life of enquiry, in which no statement should be accepted without question, and that this questioning should lead to the investigation of basic truths—the big questions. The second was that any society should be seen as a collection of different and often competing interests, and that the main task of government was to find compromises and agreements between them which would lead to the promotion of their common interests.

Hedley was also spending much time on his other subject, history. He learnt European history from Dr Bramsted, concentrating on German and French history, and the following year studied 'The Expansion of Europe', in which the rest of the world was seen as becoming part of the European empires. The fourth year course, with its emphasis on original research, was mainly Australian history, with its British background.

Hedley took part in all other activities of Arts Faculty students; he wrote to the student newspaper *Honi Soit* on a variety of subjects, was elected to the student Arts Society and became its president, co-edited the Arts Faculty magazine *Arna*, took part in many debates; and even joined, for a short spell, the Sydney University Regiment—his only military experience. He had flirted with girls from his school days, and had a succession of girlfriends in his first three years at university. When I first met him at this time, I thought him far too full of himself, and, when he told me that he liked girls who did history and philosophy, thought him patronising. But I came to realise that he was genuinely interested in what I thought on these subjects and, unlike the other male students I knew, was not merely looking for a female audience for his own views, but for a genuine discussion.

In his fourth year, 1952, life became more serious. A fourth year honours course in one subject was intended to be a full-time course; Hedley was taking two—philosophy and history—in the same year, each with a substantial thesis to be written. He moved from home to the University's Wesley College, but concentrated on work rather than its social life. He graduated at the end of the year with First Class Honours in Philosophy and Second Class Honours in History.

In the first few months of 1953 he applied for every possible position that would help towards his goal of an academic career, and was finally much relieved by the award of the University's Woolley Travelling Fellowship for study overseas. He had not applied for a Rhodes Scholarship, lacking the necessary sporting qualifications. He was accepted by University College, Oxford, to study for a B.Phil in Philosophy—a College recommended by his Sydney mentors for its philosophy tutors. (The title B.Phil., Bachelor of Philosophy, was later changed to M.Phil, as 'Master' became the generally accepted title for a second degree.) He then spent a few months working a night shift in a glass factory, making tumblers, to accumulate some money before his departure for England in August.

The Woolley Fellowship gave £400 a year for two years and, out of this, travel, university fees and all costs of living had to be paid. Hedley was fortunate that the P&O steamship line decided at this time to offer free first class passages to Australian students travelling to study in Britain. He had been considering, even before he left, whether to change his course to politics rather than philosophy, and his visits during the ship's stopovers to the universities at Melbourne, Adelaide and Perth, where he was entertained by both philosophers and political scientists, encouraged this view—and gave him useful contacts for later years. Shipboard reading of the works of the Oxford philosophers, whose doctrines of linguistic analysis had been dismissed by Anderson, decided him.

After the luxurious life aboard the SS *Strathaird* and the stops at Bombay, Aden, the Suez Canal, Marseilles and Gibraltar, Hedley at first found England to be interesting, but cold, grey and lonely. In Oxford the term had not yet begun, and his primary tasks were to find student lodgings that he could afford, to buy a bicycle, and to learn how to feed himself within his budget. The discoveries of British restaurants (where a filling meal could be had for two shillings) and youth hostels (so that he could make hitchhiking expeditions to explore the countryside) were cheering. Better was the arrival back in Oxford of students he had known from Sydney—primarily David Armstrong, a good Andersonian and later Professor of Philosophy in Sydney, and his wife Madeleine, who were helpful on practical as well as academic matters, Rawdon Dalrymple and Henry Bosch, and then the West Australian Rhodes Scholar, Bob Hawke, who were convivial evening companions. University College had no politics tutor; this had the advantage that Hedley was sent to the best tutors from other Colleges, but the disadvantage that he never spent much time at College or became friends with non-Australian students there. He came to know a number of Americans—four of the eight students studying for the B.Phil in Politics were American—and some Europeans, but few English. In March 1954 I joined him in Oxford, and we were married in the College Chapel—and in the Oxford Registry Office, since the Chapel was not legally recognised to conduct weddings. Bob Hawke lent us his van for a honeymoon tour of the Cotswolds, and we then found a flat in central Oxford's Wellington Square. I was fortunate enough to

3

obtain the position of research assistant to Margery Perham of Nuffield College, the authority on Britain's African colonies, and this provided not only an interesting occupation, but a reasonable salary. As we both had been brought up to frugal habits, Hedley never worried about money or domestic matters again.

However, he found that he had to work hard. The B.Phil course assumed that its students had done undergraduate work in politics—the politics section of the Oxford Philosophy, Politics and Economics (PPE) course, or its equivalent. Hedley had to catch up on the standard works on government and political theory. He chose to take six subjects for examination, rather than write a thesis and take fewer papers. Three basic papers in political institutions and political theory were compulsory, and his choices from the optional list included 'Theories of Law' and 'Hegel and Marx'. He did not choose the option 'International Relations'. He wrote tutorial and seminar essays, and learnt much from, among others, Isaiah Berlin, John Plamenatz, Kenneth Wheare, H.L.A. Hart, and Norman Chester, widening his outlook as well as his knowledge.

The degree of B.Phil did not have classes; students either passed or failed. So it was a genuine relief to Hedley in June 1955 to learn that he had passed. The B.Phil was then regarded as a qualification for university teaching, and doctorates were rare, although, under American influence, becoming more common. Hedley, however, did not want to spend two or three years in scholarly research, but to teach and argue amongst the students and staff of a university department. His aim was still to become an Australian academic, but he thought that a few years of teaching experience in Britain would improve his qualifications. We also wanted to see more of Europe before returning to Australia. He therefore applied for any possible academic post in Britain, even for the very unlikely one of assistant lecturer in international relations at the London School of Economics and Political Science (LSE). The post, for which he was much better qualified, assistant lecturer in political philosophy at the University of Aberdeen, was offered to him on the phone; and for two days we told everyone that we were going to Aberdeen. But then Hedley was asked to an interview at the LSE, and shortly after received a telegram from the Professor, Charles Manning, telling him that he had been appointed. The Aberdeen Professor was most understanding when Hedley rang to decline his offer—of course, he said, anyone would prefer to go to London. It was hard to believe the LSE selection—Norman Chester at Nuffield, when I told him of it, said, 'But does he feel qualified to *teach* the subject?' We learnt in time that Manning did not want lecturers who had been taught the subject of international relations by anyone else; he wanted his staff to learn his own idiosyncratic view of it. What had been most important in Hedley's selection had been the reference provided by Herbert Hart, who had tutored Hedley for the 'Theories of Law' paper. Manning had trained as a lawyer, and had for some years been law tutor at New College, where

Hart had been his pupil. Hedley's background in philosophy and history, and his recent work in political and legal theory, suited Manning's conception of what was required in his department.

So in July 1955 we packed up our Oxford flat, spent £50 on a 1936 Austin taxi, loaded it with camping gear, and with another Australian couple, Clive and Jill Wood, set out on a six-week exploration of continental Europe. Fortunately Clive was an engineer; without his daily attention the taxi would not have crossed the Channel, and certainly not the Alps. After travelling through Germany, Austria, north Italy and France, we returned in September to start a new life in London.

Twenty years later we came to live in Oxford again. Hedley had left the LSE in 1967 (having been seconded for the previous two years to the Foreign Office as head of the government's Arms Control and Disarmament Research Unit) to become Professor of International Relations at The Australian National University in Canberra. During the eight years in Canberra, he had kept in close contact with British and American scholars, travelling each year to the northern hemisphere, with a visit of up to six weeks in September which enabled him to attend meetings and conferences of the International Institute of Strategic Studies and the British Committee on the Theory of International Politics. Study leave in 1970–71 was spent by all the family—now including children of six, four and one—at Columbia University in New York, and in London at the LSE and the IISS. The next study leave was split into two parts, October 1974–February 1975 at Jawaharlal Nehru University in Delhi, and then October1975–July1976 as a Visiting Fellow at All Souls College, Oxford. Oxford had become a more attractive university for the study of international relations with the appointment of Alastair Buchan as Professor of International Relations in 1972, and the move of Michael Howard as Fellow in Higher Defence Studies and in 1977 as Professor of the History of War, both posts at All Souls. He was able to arrange for Hedley to become a Visiting Fellow, with a flat in North Oxford to accommodate the family, and we began the year as temporary visitors from Australia. But in February 1976, Alastair Buchan suddenly and tragically died. Hedley did not want to leave Canberra, where we had settled so happily, but he did realise the advantages to his study of international relations of being in a major world centre, and especially as an Oxford professor. So he applied for the Montague Burton Chair of International Relations, and it was on our way back to Canberra, holidaying for a few days in Venice, that he received a telegram from Michael Howard to say that he had been elected.

So our last eight months in Canberra were spent in preparations for leaving. We did not regard it as necessarily a permanent departure; we arranged to let our house, not to sell it. In April 1977 we moved once more to Oxford, and bought a house in North Oxford; fortunately the schools that the children had been attending the previous year were able to take them back. The International Relations professor was also a fellow of Balliol College, so Hedley was given a room there, and had to learn the ways of the College; though there was also a faculty building where he shared a secretary. He lunched in College most days, appreciating the opportunity for discussions with those outside his immediate fields of study—one of these was the philosopher, and later Master of Balliol, Anthony Kenny.

Professors in Oxford supervise graduate students, while College Fellows teach undergraduates. Alastair Buchan had done much to attract graduate students to the new B.Phil (soon renamed M.Phil) in international relations, as well as for doctorates; and the numbers of students admitted rose steadily. Some of these graduate students could be supervised by other professors, especially Michael Howard, but most were supervised by College tutors in politics who were interested in international relations, such as Wilfrid Knapp, John Dunbabin, Christopher Seton-Watson and Peter Pulzer. However, the first priority of College tutors was to the undergraduates of their College—mostly to those taking the optional PPE paper on international relations. Hedley was anxious to create more posts whose holders could concentrate on the graduate students, and over the next eight years he raised funds and persuaded the university and the graduate Colleges to create an Alastair Buchan Reader, and an economic Fellow at St Antony's, and, with the help of the Ford Foundation, a University Lectureship in international relations at Nuffield College—the first holder of this, shortly after Hedley's death, was John Vincent, whom he had taught in Canberra, and who had become a good friend in the subsequent years when John was at Keele University. Adam Roberts moved from the LSE to become the Alastair Buchan Reader in 1981, and did much to make life easier for Hedley. He continued, however, to supervise a large number of graduate students, in whom he took great interest. Committee meetings took up a great deal of time, but the one committee which he was always made sure of attending was that which decided the admissions to the graduate degrees. There were always many more applicants than there were places on the M.Phil course, and he made sure of being involved, even when nominally on study leave, in selecting those whom he thought to be the best. One of the advantages of teaching at Oxford, he said, was that it attracted the best students from around the world, and he was stimulated by and learnt much from them.

The other obligation of an Oxford professor was to give at least six lectures each term—though for one term it was permissible to conduct a seminar, which Hedley normally organised for the third term; he also collaborated in seminars in the earlier terms. For the first term he alternated his two sets of standard lectures on the theory and the history of international relations, so that M.Phil students could hear both in their two years; in the second term he lectured on the subject on which he was currently working—for, he said, the best way of making himself undertake the reading and develop his thoughts on a subject was to put himself down to lecture on it. In this way he worked on what was to be the book, co-edited with Adam Watson, *The Expansion of International Society*, and what was planned to be a following volume on *The Revolt against Western Dominance*. He also wanted to write on the history of international thought, and was collecting material and lecturing on writers dealing with the history and the events of their times from sixteenth to twentieth century Europe. He spent a considerable time preparing each lecture, and then took pride in delivering them without notes.

He also organised lecture series. In Hilary term 1982 he arranged eight lectures by international experts on the topic of 'Intervention in World Politics' and, with the addition of an introduction and a chapter of his own, they were published with this title in 1984. In 1983 he arranged for a series of lectures in honour of Adam von Trott, the German Rhodes Scholar who was executed in 1944 for his part in the plot against Hitler, in conjunction with Balliol College, where von Trott had studied, and David Astor, who had been his contemporary there. These were edited by Hedley and published in 1986 under the title *The Challenge of the Third Reich: The Adam von Trott Memorial Lectures*. In Michaelmas term 1983 he arranged a lecture series to mark the quatercentenary of the birth of Hugo Grotius. This series took longer to organise into a book, with several additional chapters commissioned, and was not published until 1990, after Hedley's death, as *Hugo Grotius and International Relations*, edited by Hedley Bull, Adam Roberts and Benedict Kingsbury. In 1984–85 he worked with Wm. Roger Louis to hold a series of conferences, sponsored by the Ditchley Foundation in Oxfordshire, and the Woodrow Wilson International Center in Washington, on Anglo-American Relations since the Second World War. These were published, with them both as joint editors, as *The Special Relationship* in 1986.

There were also meetings in London. He tried to keep Thursdays free of Oxford commitments as that was the day of most meetings of the IISS, of which he was on the Council, and of Chatham House, where he was for some years Director of Research. He was also on the Board of the Australian Studies Institute of the University of London, and a member of the Round Table, which studied Commonwealth affairs. But most time and thought went to the British Committee on the Theory of International Politics. This group of theorists of international relations was undergoing changes, and Hedley worked with Adam Watson to engage in a new project—the study of the expansion of European international society. The usual program was to hold weekend meetings—originally at Peterhouse, Cambridge, chaired by its Master, Herbert Butterfield, but now also in other universities, including Oxford. Members and guests contributed papers on relevant aspects of the spread of the European states system, and Hedley and Adam wrote an introduction and conclusion, as well as their own chapters. The jointly edited book, *The Expansion of International Society*, was published by Oxford University Press in 1984.

In vacations, it seemed that he was always travelling to conferences and other meetings. He made many visits to the United States, and to Europe—Eastern as well as Western—and some to Australia and Asia. In the Easter vacation of 1984 he spent several weeks in South America. He had not previously been there, except for a conference in Chile on the Pacific Rim in 1970, and felt he should know more of the continent and its scholars. However, we did manage a family holiday each summer, most in Greece, in Corfu and Crete, for we all felt the need of beaches and sunshine. Swimming and snorkelling were still his favourite pastimes.

Chapter 2

An Early Influence: John Anderson

Renée Jeffery

Introduction

An Australian by birth and, in many ways character, Hedley Bull stands as one of the most prominent theorists of twentieth century British international relations.[1] The author of the highly regarded 1977 work *The Anarchical Society: A Study of Order in World Politics*, Bull is most commonly characterised as standing alongside Martin Wight as one of the most prominent members of the so-called 'English School' of international relations.[2] In particular, much has been made in recent scholarship of the extent to which Bull was influenced by Wight, Tim Dunne's history of the 'English School' noting that Bull not only stands in a pattern of intellectual lineage that extends from Wight to Bull's student R.J. Vincent, but 'thought about International Relations in quintessentially Wightean terms'.[3]

In large part, this impression is derived from Bull's own assessment of his intellectual development. In particular, Bull is known to have attended Wight's famous lecture series as a junior academic at the London School of Economics (LSE) in the mid-1950s and readily admitted that the experience exerted a 'profound impression' upon him. Bull even went so far as to write that he 'felt in the shadow of Martin Wight's thought—humbled by it, a constant borrower from it, always hoping to transcend it but never able to escape from it'.[4] Similarly, the preface of his most famous work, *The Anarchical Society*, speaks of the 'profound debt' Bull felt he owed Wight for demonstrating to him 'that International Relations could be made a subject'.[5]

However, alongside Wight, a number of other figures have also been credited with influencing Bull's intellectual development. Among the most prominent stand H.L.A. Hart,[6] one of the most important legal theorists of the twentieth century who taught Bull during his time at Oxford, and C.A.W. Manning, the figure responsible for appointing him to his first assistant lectureship at the LSE.[7] What is somewhat surprising is that the influence of John Anderson, Bull's teacher at the University of Sydney, has not been afforded sustained consideration in much international relations scholarship. Indeed, although intellectual histories of Bull's thought occasionally mention in passing that Anderson must be considered one of his foremost influences, this association has not been afforded the attention it rightly warrants in thinking about the history of ideas in British international relations.[8] What makes this omission particularly surprising is Bull's explicit acknowledgement of Anderson's influence in the preface to *The Anarchical Society*:

> My greatest intellectual debt is to John Anderson ... a greater man than many who are more famous. He had little to say directly about the matters discussed in this book, but the impact of his mind and his example has been the deepest factor in shaping the outlook of many of us whom he taught.[9]

The Challis Chair of Philosophy at the University of Sydney from 1927 to 1958, John Anderson was, in David Armstrong's view, 'the most important philosopher who has worked in Australia'.[10] A Scot by birth and educated at the University of Glasgow, Anderson's move to Australia was, as John Passmore writes, 'the greatest piece of intellectual good fortune our country has ever experienced'.[11] Although he only published one book during his lifetime, *Education and Politics*—three editions of collected articles and lectures, *Studies in Empirical Philosophy*; *Education and Inquiry*; and *Art and Reality* have been published posthumously while his *Lecture Notes and Other Writings* have been made available on-line—his influence extended to a number of realms.[12] In the field of philosophy, Anderson expounded the merits of what A.J. (Jim) Baker has termed 'Australian realism', a form of extreme philosophical realism, at a time when idealism was still the dominant mode of thought in Australian philosophy.[13] A 'theoretical advisor' to the Communist Party of Australia and later associate of the United Front Against Fascism, Friends of the Soviet Union, and the Trotskyist Workers Party, Anderson was also well known for his socialist sentiments. In Australian society, Anderson is best remembered as a public controversialist who twice instigated censure motions in the New South Wales and Federal parliaments for his outspoken views on censorship, war memorials, sexual liberation, and the role of religion in education.[14] However, it was among his students that he exerted the greatest influence. Indeed, even critics among his former students acknowledge Anderson's impact on their intellectual development. For example, David Stove once wrote that '[t]he influence Anderson exercised was purely, or as purely as a human influence can be, purely intellectual. I never felt anything like the force of his intellect'.[15]

With this in mind, this chapter therefore seeks to assess precisely what the 'intellectual debt' Bull felt he owed to Anderson might be. It begins by further introducing the figure of John Anderson, focusing in particular on his teaching style and views on the role of the academic. The second section then goes on to outline what has become known in philosophical circles as 'Australian realism', Anderson's particular mix of pluralism, empiricism and positivism, before considering the implications of his philosophical thought for his understandings of the nature of ethical inquiry, the role of religion in education and the functioning of human society. The second half of the chapter then turns to the thought of Hedley Bull and considers the influence of Anderson in three areas of Bull's thought: his general approach to the study and teaching of international relations; his understanding of international society, in particular his pluralist outlook; and the scepticism with which he approached religious ideas and certain forms of moral thought. The chapter concludes by suggesting that although he deviates from Anderson's more extreme criticisms of ethical inquiry, Bull's general approach to the study of international relations, pluralist understanding of international society and, in particular, sceptical attitude towards religion were certainly consistent with the teachings of his earliest mentor. Interestingly, it is also with regard to these issues that Bull's position was furthest from his more commonly acknowledged intellectual influence, Martin Wight.

John Anderson (1893–1962)

Anderson's style, it has often been noted, was both Socratic and authoritarian.[16] As Peter Shrubb, one of Anderson's former students, remarked in an article that appeared shortly after Anderson's death:

> Here, shivering, my Philosophy I class sat on the morning of March 20, 1945, waiting to hear its first lecture from Professor Anderson. This was the introduction to a series on the Apology, Socrates' defence at his trial, and before it was half over I already had the bull by the foot; I was young and fodish, and I was not sure which was Socrates and which was John Anderson. One was short, strikingly ugly, and wore a sort of toga; the other was tall, strikingly handsome, and wore a blue suit. But these differences were superficial. They were great men, and men of the same kind.[17]

Following in the Socratic style, Anderson maintained that '[t]he work of the academic, qua academic is criticism'.[18] In this vein, John Passmore has gone so far as to suggest that, with the exception of his writings on logic and, to some degree ethics, 'Anderson did not develop his views systematically but rather through a critique of the classical philosophers'.[19] He was not, in Passmore's view, 'a scholar' of the classic texts, but relied on secondary interpretations, and focused on critique as the basis of his scholarship.[20] Indeed, his ability to critique and 'powers of dismissal were simply boundless'.[21]

This critical focus was also reflected in Anderson's teaching style. 'Socratic education begins', he wrote in an early article, 'with the awakening of the mind to the need for criticism, to the uncertainty of the principles by which it supposed itself to be guided'.[22] That said, among the most often repeated criticisms of Anderson's scholarly style is that he could not tolerate being criticised himself. He was, as Armstrong notes, 'authoritarian in his own personality and intolerant of dissent from his own views among his staff and students'.[23] His greatest intellectual weakness was his overwhelming desire to acquire disciples, many of his former students noting that they were treated with suspicion by Anderson for not joining the inner circle of his followers.[24]

Anderson's authoritarian nature was also reflected in his lecturing style; his lectures were dictated in what were 'by formal standards' the 'worst possible' manner.[25] As tedious as it must have been for his students to endure this 'pedagogical passivity',[26] the distinct advantage of Anderson's method for contemporary scholars is that his lecture notes represent almost exactly what was conveyed to his students. It is thus from his lecture notes and other papers, particularly 'Realism and Some of its Critics',[27] that we can begin to discern precisely what Anderson's 'Australian realism' entailed.

Australian Realism

In general terms, philosophical realism is comprised of three fundamental principles. Its first and central claim 'maintains the independence of the known from the knowing of it'.[28] That is, it is an ontological position that claims that objects exist even if no one is conscious of them or experiences them. Secondly, philosophical realism maintains that what we know is known to us through observation. This ultimately means it is fundamentally opposed to rationalism and, in particular, knowledge derived through the process of deduction. Finally, and following from its epistemological standpoint, philosophical realism also claims that the only appropriate method according to which such knowledge is to be attained is that of empiricism.

In both its political and philosophical forms, realism emerged in response to the dominant mode of thought in both fields in the early twentieth century, idealism. As John Passmore writes, during the time when Anderson studied there, the University of Glasgow 'was still an outpost of Absolute Idealism'.[29] 'Absolute' Hegelian idealism had been established as the dominant mode of philosophical thought at Glasgow by Edward Caird whose influence stretched to the philosophy schools of Australia.[30] Its central claim was that 'ordinary things or "outside objects" (apart from other minds) depend for their existence on being known'. That is, idealists claim that 'reality is experience'.[31] Thus objects, such as 'tables, buildings, mountains and so on' do not exist if no one is conscious of them or experiences them.[32] This, of course, is in direct opposition to the realist claim that whatever exists does so regardless of whether or not anyone is conscious of it.

Although he was not the first philosopher to oppose idealism in Australia—Bernard Muscio, the Challis Professor immediately prior to Anderson was a formidable critic of the approach[33]—it was Anderson who finally turned the tide, at the University of Sydney at least. Indeed, as we will see shortly,

Anderson's realism cut directly to the heart of idealist thought, challenging its fundamental premise at the outset. Foremost among Anderson's primary influences in this endeavour were the 'modern realists', G.E. Moore and Bertrand Russell, and the American 'new realists', W.T. Marvin, R.B. Perry and Samuel Alexander. In particular, Anthony Quinton writes that 'a powerful influence was exerted on him by the Gifford Lectures delivered ... by Samuel Alexander, later published as *Time, Space and Deity*'.[34] Significantly, in the preface to *The Anarchical Society*, Bull wrote: 'When still an undergraduate I was very impressed (I now think too impressed) by the dictum of Samuel Alexander, the author of *Time, Space and Deity* ... that "thinking is also research"'.[35] As we will see shortly, Anderson's understanding of philosophical realism was fundamentally based on Alexander's doctrine of spatio-temporality.[36] However, as we will also see in the following section, where Anderson made his own contribution to realist philosophical thought was in the manner in which he developed its empirical approach into 'a logical and propositional account of reality as a theory of discourse about events'.[37]

Empiricism, Pluralism and Positivism

As Anderson wrote in 'Realism and Some of its Critics', although 'we cannot define Realism by what any particular realist says', it is possible to identify three principles, or sets of ideas that are constitutive of his particular brand of the approach.[38] In accordance with the general definition provided above, for Anderson, realism was an empiricist doctrine that maintained, at its heart, that existence is 'the single way of being'.[39] More specifically, Anderson maintained that 'everything that there is exists in time and space', a contention derived directly from Alexander's doctrine of spatio-temporality.[40] Realism, for Anderson, was consequently concerned with 'being real' and by extension he argued that 'being real' 'should be unambiguous' so as to avoid all notions pertaining to 'orders' of reality.[41] That is, he argued that 'whatever exists ... is real, that is to say it is a spatio and temporal situation or occurrence that is on the same level of reality as anything else that exists'.[42] This position, often referred to as Anderson's 'ontological egalitarianism', stands in direct opposition to both idealism and rationalism and, in doing so, takes the general ontological claim made by philosophical realism to its logical extreme. Indeed, despite arguing with Hume and Mill that 'experience is the only guide to what is the case', in the final analysis Anderson rejected their positions as being ultimately 'rationalistic'.[43] Thus, Anderson went so far as to promulgate the extreme empiricist position that 'a realist can only be an empiricist'.[44] In doing so, he thus fused the ontological claim that everything that exists does so regardless of whether anyone is conscious of it, with the epistemological claim that what we know is known to us through observation, and discussed them under the broad banner of empiricism.

The two remaining principles of 'Australian realism' follow from Anderson's extreme empiricist position. The first is the claim that realism is a pluralistic doctrine. This, as Jim Baker writes, was to be defended in Anderson's view 'as a matter of fact'.[45] As Passmore explains, for Anderson, 'every fact (which includes every "object") is a complex situation: there are no simples, no atomic facts, no objects which cannot be, as it were, expanded into facts'.[46] That is, Anderson 'affirm[ed] "the infinite complexity of things" and denie[d] that there is anything absolutely simple, anything less than a complex situation'.[47] As we will see shortly, this notion of complexity that was central to Anderson's understanding of pluralism was derived, at least in part, from his fascination with Heraclitus and also informed his social thought.

Finally, and also following from his extreme empiricism, Anderson maintained that realism is a 'positivist doctrine'.[48] However, by positivism he did not mean 'logical positivism' for this was, in his view, 'thoroughly rationalistic' in nature.[49] Rather, Anderson understood positivism as a methodological approach centred around the empirical observation of objects and events. This, somewhat curiously, also included ethical inquiry.

Ethics

In accordance with his empiricist and positivist understanding of realism, for Anderson, ethics must necessarily be concerned with 'facts'. As such, he maintained that 'there are no "values" above facts'.[50] Rather, ethics must be treated in the same manner as any other social phenomena; that is to say, positively. This, of course, is in direct contradiction to the more common understanding of ethics as being concerned not simply with the principles of human conduct but with how human beings ought to act; that is, with the normative element of ethical inquiry. However, Anderson went so far as to suggest that 'there is no such thing as a "normative" science'.[51] According to Anderson, 'the most obstinate confusion obstructing the growth of ethical knowledge lies in the assumption that ethics teaches us how to live or what to live for, that it instructs us in our duty or in the approach to the moral end'.[52]

This view accords directly with Anderson's understanding of what it is to be a 'freethinker'.[53] As he wrote in 'The Nature of Freethought',[54] the 'freethinker' is a 'disinterested theorist', not in the sense of being opposed to the interested theorist, but in the sense of maintaining 'that theory has nothing to do with betterment'. This, of course, rests on a fundamental distinction between 'positive science', one of the hallmarks of Anderson's Freethought Society, and normative inquiry. However, Anderson also argued that the very distinction between 'what is' and 'what ought to be' that marks the positivist/normative divide is fundamentally illogical. Its illogicality, he argued, stems from 'its conception of the different sorts of reality which attach to norms and to the things which come under these norms'.[55] That is, it stems from the 'attempt to distinguish facts from values'. In accordance with Anderson's empiricist and positivist understanding of realism however, 'if the statement that something "ought to be" has any meaning, it can only be that the thing is, positively obligatory; that this is a matter of fact'.[56] This, of course, is because Anderson did not believe that different levels of reality can be identified; rather, everything that exists is as real as everything else that exists. For Anderson then, 'good is a matter of discoverable natural fact' and does not have anything whatsoever to do with how an individual ought to behave or think or what ought to happen in a given situation.

It is possible to identify two immediate implications of this view. The first, which I will return to in the following discussion of Anderson's views about religion, is that he was outwardly hostile towards 'moralism'. 'Moralism' was, in Anderson's view, a 'fraud' because it brought with it a false sense of obligation.[57] The second implication of Anderson's positivist view of ethics is the claim that not only is there 'no such thing as the common good' and no need to pursue moral or social progress, but that there is 'perhaps no possibility of it' occurring at all.[58] This has specific implications for Anderson's understanding of both society and religion.

Religion

Anderson's hostility towards religion is almost legendary in Australian society and scholarship. Although he initially rejected religion on Comtean grounds, Anderson's later criticisms of it were made on 'both ethical and logical grounds'. In agreement with Nietzsche and in accordance 'with his positive theory of ethics he regard[ed] Christianity ... as essentially servile and philanthropic in its outlook and preoccupations ... and so as quite opposed to what is intrinsically good'.[59] Focusing his criticisms on Christianity in particular, he argued that 'the Christian ethic, as an ethic of renunciation and consolation, as holding out to the lowly on earth in expectation of "elevation" in some unearthly sense, stands low in the scale of moralities'.[60] In particular, Christianity brings with it, he argued, an implicit and unsubstantiated claim to a higher form of morality.[61] Christianity is thus 'a feudal attitude which is characterised by social helplessness' and presents a 'mere veneer of solidarity in its emphasis on acquiescence to oppression and its doctrine of personal salvation'.[62] On logical grounds, Anderson also argued that 'theology (is) not only an ambiguous doctrine of reality, (it) is also an ambiguous position itself'. It cannot be, he maintained, treated as an aspect of science or even philosophy but can only be reduced to an aspect of social science, one of many facets of human history.[63]

However, Anderson's complaint with religion was not simply a general one but was specifically directed towards the role of religion in education, the subject of one of the public controversies in which he found himself. Indeed, Anderson famously argued in his 1943 speech 'Religion in Education', 'as with the subject of snakes in Ireland there is no religion in education'. 'Education', he argued, 'may be described as the development of inquiry, the setting up of habits of investigation'. Religion, he continued, is thus 'opposed to education' because that which is 'sacred' is, by definition, immune to inquiry, examination and criticism. 'To call anything sacred', he argued, 'is to say, "Here inquiry must stop; this is not to be examined"'.[64]

Society

Like his views on religion and ethics more generally, Anderson's social critique was fundamentally based on the empiricist and pluralist elements of his philosophical realism. In general terms, this meant that Anderson rejected what 'he regarded as fundamental misconceptions in social science'; specifically the 'confused doctrines of voluntarism, individualism or social atomism, and solidarism'.[65] Indeed, the logical corollary of Anderson's argument against moralism discussed above was his rejection of solidarism, the view that society is a 'solid or harmonious thing, or a single whole' in which all 'members have a common set of interests'.[66] This, Anderson argued, is an illusion that is based on false notions of the common good and 'neglects the fact of social variety and social conflict, that is, the fact of social pluralism'.[67] However, this did not mean that Anderson disregarded all notions of 'co-operation and social cohesion' in his understanding of society, but rather maintained that 'these are not the dominant social facts as conflict and struggle are permanent important features of society and history'.[68] Indeed, conflict was central to Anderson's understanding of society and this was derived, at least in part, from his interest in the pre-Socratic Greek philosopher, Heraclitus.

As I.F. Helu argues, 'Anderson saw in Heraclitus's doctrine three basic ideas: process, tension, and complexity'.[69] In particular, it was Heraclitus' specific notion of the 'complexity and permanence of conflict and change in any situation, natural or social' that most interested Anderson.[70] Indeed, as Heraclitus wrote, emphasising the place of conflict in society: 'We must recognise that war is common and strife is justice, and all things happen according to strife and necessity.'[71] Anderson's sympathetic view of Heraclitus is made evident in his 1960 paper 'Classicism':

> Heraclitus, who was unremitting in his attack on subjectivist illusions, on the operation of desire or the imagining of things as we should like them to be, as opposed to the operation or understanding of the finding of things (including our own activities) as they positively are—his criticism was directed especially against the school of the

Pythagoreans—against their distortion of their material from a desire for simplicity, for the tidy and complete solution.[72]

Thus, Anderson saw in Heraclitus a call to realism, positivism and complexity and a critique of normative aspirations.

However, Anderson's understanding of the inherently conflictual nature of society was also a function of his Marxism. In particular, along with following Marx's 'atheism, secularism and determinism', he also accepted 'his view of class struggle' and of the existence of 'irreconcilable antagonisms in society'.[73] At the same time however, Anderson repudiated Marxism's 'monism, its teleological view of history and its utopianism'.[74] Indeed, despite the passion with which he adhered to Marx's ideas about society early in his career, by the 1940s Anderson had begun to argue that society is comprised not simply of class divisions but 'a diversity of movements such as Church, State and trade unions, which cannot be reduced to a class theory of society'.[75] In accordance with his pluralist outlook then, what underpinned Anderson's interest in such diverse social movements was the observation, not simply that a community of interests—such as that implied by the class theory of society—did not exist, but that it was not possible.

Despite his emphasis on divergent interests and conflict however, Anderson did leave some room for cooperation in his understanding of society. In particular, he argued that institutions ultimately mitigate the effects of pluralism. As John Passmore notes, Anderson believed that the question to be asked of any social institution was not 'What end or purpose does it serve?' but 'Of what conflicts is it the scene?'[76] For Anderson then, institutions were conceived as 'forms of activity' that represent 'specific interests' and are bound together through the 'communication' of their participants, this allowing them to find 'common ways of working' or common 'forms of activity'. As such, social movements and institutions are ultimately 'communication centres' in Anderson's view.[77] Despite the existence of these 'common ways of working' however, Anderson maintained that neither the identification of a broader community of interests nor the recognition of universal values is possible. As we will see in the following section, this argument against universalism is also replicated in the work of Hedley Bull.

Hedley Bull (1932–85)

Hedley Bull graduated from the University of Sydney with a Bachelor of Arts with Honours in Philosophy in 1952 before heading to Oxford to study for a B.Phil. in Politics. As mentioned above, it was as a young academic at the LSE that Bull came into contact with Martin Wight, the figure most often attributed with influencing his intellectual development. Despite Wight's impact on Bull however, it is also possible to identify a number of significant points of divergence between his thought and that of Bull, particularly in relation to questions of religion and ethics in international society. As Ian Hall notes, throughout his life Wight was 'a fervent and rather traditionalist Anglican',[78] his religious faith exerting a significant impact upon his own treatment of international relations. This, however, was a source of great consternation for Bull who admitted in 'Martin Wight and the Theory of International Relations' that he often 'felt uneasy about the extent to which Wight's view of International Relations derived from his religious beliefs'.[79] As we will see shortly however, Bull's views on religion and ethics accorded well with those of his earliest mentor, John Anderson. In particular, Bull's time at the University of Sydney coincided with Anderson's 'religion in education' phase. Indeed, Bull is acknowledged, albeit for his misunderstanding of Anderson's position, in the 1950 lecture 'The Nature of Freethought':

> Hedley Bull's 'defence' of me says that I give an initial training in logic which is NON-Christian (not anti-Christian) and then state my conclusions (which *are* anti-Christian) and the student may disagree and criticise. But I do not 'state', but *draw* conclusions. I show that what follows from premises I assume anyone will accept.

The influence of Anderson on Bull also extended to other aspects of Bull's thought and style. As Michael Howard has noted: 'It was from Anderson that [Bull] learned that a combination of open-mindedness in approach and rigour in analysis which was to distinguish him throughout his career and which he would in due time pass on to his own pupils.'[80] Bull also shared with Anderson a sceptical mind and an 'abrasive and arrogant manner'.[81]

Like Anderson, Bull was also renowned for his Socratic style. As James Richardson wrote, 'amongst the qualities he prized most were the Socratic questioning of received opinion', adding later that 'in his commitment to the Socratic pursuit of the argument irrespective of where it might lead, his sharp eye for illusion and rationalisation, his suspicion of orthodoxies, and his scorn for superficiality, Bull remained quintessentially Andersonian'.[82] Also following in Anderson's footsteps Bull was, as Don Markwell wrote, 'a master of demolition'.[83] 'Remorseless in criticism',[84] Bull believed that the 'enterprise of theoretical investigation is at its minimum one directed towards criticism'.[85] Unlike Anderson however, Bull was 'highly receptive to other people's impressions of his own work'.[86] Also deviating from Anderson, Bull's lecturing style was, as a former student wrote, 'impressive, even dazzling'.[87]

Despite some differences in character and style however, Bull made many elements of Anderson's approach 'his own and applied it rigorously',[88] going so far as to suggest that 'none could apply [Anderson's] precepts better than Bull'. In particular, Bull held firmly to the empiricism that Anderson had promulgated. As he explained in 'International Theory: The Case for the Classical

Approach', this did not amount to a 'strict' empiricism of the sort adhered to by proponents of the 'scientific approach to international relations theory',[89] but was rather understood in the manner Anderson had intended. In particular, it is in the following statement that Bull's empiricism and general philosophical realism is evident:

> Theoretical inquiry into an empirical subject normally proceeds by way of the assertion of general connections and distinctions between events in the real world. But it is the practice of many of these writers to cast their theories in the form of a deliberately simplified abstraction from reality, which they then turn over and examine this way and that before considering what modifications must be effected if it is to be applied to the real world.[90]

Aside from the general criticisms he leveled at proponents of the 'scientific approach' for the extent to which their ideas were abstracted from reality, Bull was particularly concerned with the deductive reasoning central to the construction of models favoured by this approach. 'The virtue that is supposed to lie in models', he wrote, 'is that [of] liberating us from the restraint of constant reference to reality'.[91] However, as he continued:

> The freedom of the model-builder from the discipline of looking at the world is what makes him dangerous; he slips easily into a dogmatism that empirical generalisation does not allow, attributing to the model a connection with reality it does not have, and as often as not distorting the model itself by importing additional assumptions about the world in the guise of logical axioms. The very intellectual completeness and logical tidiness of the model-building operation lends it an air of authority which is often quite misleading as to its standing as a statement about the real world.[92]

However, not only was Bull a philosophical realist and empiricist but, also in accordance with Anderson, a positivist. As Maurice Keens-Soper once remarked to Martin Wight regarding an argument he had had with Bull over the nature of historical facts: 'He, for goodness sake, turns out to be a positivist, at least in this matter. He maintained that historical facts were in principle no different from the 'facts' which our senses give us.'[93]

International Society

Although the Marxist elements of Anderson's understanding of society did not accord well with Bull's thought, other aspects of his teachings appear in Bull's discussions of international society. International society, according to Bull, is defined in general terms as

> a group of states, conscious of common interests and common values, [who] form a society in the sense that they conceive themselves to be bound by a common set of rules in their relations with one another, and share in the workings of common institutions.

States form an 'international society', he contended

> because, recognising certain common interests and perhaps some common values, they regard themselves as bound by certain rules in their dealings with one another, such as that they should respect one another's claims to independence, that they should honour agreements into which they enter, and that they should be subject to certain limitations in exercising force against one another.[94]

It is possible to identify two particularly Andersonian elements in this understanding of international society. First, although they all appear to be normative criteria for the formation of international society, the recognition of common interests and values and so on are actually positive in orientation. That is, states do not recognise that they ought to develop common interests and values; they recognise that they do have common interests and values and form institutions accordingly. What is more, Bull maintains that states 'should respect one another's claims to independence' and so on, not because it is an ideal aspiration for the future, but because these principles represent the conditions according to which international society is actually formed. In this, despite appearing on the surface to be presenting an explicitly normative understanding of international society, Bull actually came extremely close to presenting the sort of positivist conception that Anderson was in favour of.

Second, Bull's understanding of institutions, particularly when coupled with his view that international politics is fundamentally anarchical in nature, accords well with Anderson's discussions of social institutions. Thus, the recognition of common interests and values in Bull's definition of international society equates to the 'specific interests' of which Anderson spoke, while the manner in which states work together in common institutions and share certain rules in their dealings with one another represent two 'forms of activity' central to Anderson's understanding of institutions. In particular, the 'tension' that Stanley Hoffman notes in Bull's thought between 'his realism and his emphasis on the rules and institutions which dampen anarchy'[95] is reminiscent of Anderson's discussions of society. These things aside however, it was with his discussions of pluralism in international society that Bull veered even closer to Anderson's view.

In 'The Grotian Conception of International Society' Bull identified and distinguished between two approaches to the concept of international society, pluralism and solidarism. Recognising the multiple conceptions of justice that operate in international relations, pluralism is 'a conception of international society founded upon the observation of the actual area of agreement between states and informed by a sense of the limitations within which this situation rules may usefully be made rules of law'.[96] In the work of João Marques de Almeida, the positivist focus of this understanding of pluralism is attributed to the influence of H.L.A. Hart, although it also accords very well with the pluralist and positivist principles of Anderson's understanding of realism.[97] Indeed, although it may also reflect the legal positivism of a 'minimal Hartian position', the claim that we must focus on the actual area of agreement between states, determined by observation, is distinctly Andersonian in sentiment. As we will see shortly, it is this approach to international society that Bull defended over the alternative he discussed, solidarism.

Contrary to pluralism, solidarism posits that international society is 'a society formed by states and sovereigns' whose position 'is secondary to that of the universal community of mankind'. The central assumption of solidarism is 'that of the solidarity, or potential solidarity, of most states in the world in upholding the collective will of the society of states against challenges to it'.[98] It consequently stands in direct opposition to the pluralist view that states 'are capable of agreeing only for certain minimal purposes which fall short of the enforcement of the law'.[99] What is more, by entertaining pretensions to the 'potential solidarity' of states, solidarism moves away from the positivist orientation of pluralism towards a more normatively oriented focus.

It is in Bull's criticisms of the solidarist position and defence of pluralism that his proximity to Anderson's teachings on positivism, pluralism and empiricism is particularly apparent. Bull was critical of solidarism for two main reasons. The first was the claim that solidarism has exerted 'an influence positively detrimental to international order … by imposing upon international society a strain that it cannot bear'. This 'strain' has resulted from the imposition of what is actually a false sense of solidarity of interests that, far from strengthening international society, 'has the effect of undermining those structures of the system which might otherwise be secure'.[100] Here Bull seems to be echoing Anderson's arguments against the supposed solidarity of human societies.[101] However, the echo becomes much louder indeed when Bull launches his further attack on solidarism's notion of the common good in international ethics.

Ethics

Bull's second complaint with the solidarist approach to international society was derived from his well-documented moral scepticism. As O'Neill and Schwartz write, Bull's 'scepticism had been nurtured by … a renowned sceptic and iconoclast', John Anderson.[102] Referring to the moral pluralism that coloured his view of international society, Stanley Hoffman has also noted that Bull was 'painfully aware of the multiplicity of moral perspectives'[103] and, as a result, viewed with immense scepticism the assertion that any form of common morality, implied by the central concepts of the solidarist approach, can be identified in international relations. This scepticism is particularly displayed in his critique of E.B.F. Midgley's *The Natural Law Tradition and the Theory of International Relations*,[104] which he described as 'dauntingly massive and impressively learned, if [an] avowedly dogmatic and profoundly reactionary attempt to rehabilitate the Thomist philosophy of natural law'.[105] Revealing his outward discomfort with the avowedly Christian elements of Midgley's work, Bull particularly criticised his 'reliance on Christian revelation, his statement that the fundamental principles of his work are confirmed by the authority of the Church and his view that natural law cannot effectively be upheld today except by theists'.[106] However, Bull's most substantial criticism of Midgley's work centered around his presentation of 'moral issues in terms of "antinomies and paradoxes"'.[107] In particular, he argued, in accordance with Anderson and contrary to Midgley, that moral questions can only be answered 'by reference to moral rules whose validity we assume'; that is, according to empirically verifiable argument.[108] These views on religion, morality and natural law certainly put him at odds with his fellow members of the 'English School', in particular, Martin Wight.

Similarly, Bull's critical approach to notions of common morality was also displayed in his review article of Michael Walzer's 1977 book *Just and Unjust Wars: A Moral Argument with Historical Illustrations*. In particular, Bull argued that, at heart, Walzer's work rested on the implicit assumption that his readers 'share[d] a common morality with him'. This, Bull argued, led Walzer to assume that he did not need to 'defend his basic moral principles', but that he could simply assert them.[109] However, as Bull pointed out later in the article, this was not the case for most of Walzer's arguments were, in his view, 'vulnerable' to attack from a variety of other positions.[110] Thus, while Bull praised Walzer's 'dismissal of relativist arguments', he also criticised his apparent 'subjectivity'.[111] For example, Bull maintained that Walzer's 'basic proposition that—as against General Sherman's doctrine that "war is hell"—the distinction between just and unjust war is of cardinal importance, would be disputed by absolute pacificists [sic], with whose position he makes no attempt to come to grips'.[112] The assumptions implicit in Walzer's argument did not amount simply to the endorsement of a notion of common morality in Bull's view, but represented the further claim that Western liberal values about the morality of war and the rights and duties of individual human beings are held universally. With Anderson, Bull disputed these very premises.

Despite Anderson's influence and the effort with which Bull criticised the solidarist approach in *The Anarchical Society* and 'The Grotian Conception of International Society', a distinct shift towards this position can be discerned in his later works. Nicholas Wheeler and Tim Dunne attempt to reconcile this move by characterising Bull as harbouring a 'pluralism of the intellect and solidarism of the will'.[113] In particular, they argue that 'later Bull came to express increasing disillusionment with pluralism on the grounds that it could not provide for order among states and hence order among the wider society of humankind'.[114] Evidence of this growing disillusionment first began to appear in the early 1980s and, in particular, the Hagey Lectures of 1983. Here, despite his previous arguments against the solidarist approach, Bull discussed the notion of a 'growing cosmopolitan awareness' in international relations.[115] Furthermore, he also began to discuss the 'concept of a world common good' and argued that. 'in the absence of a supranational world authority'. the need existed 'for particular states to seek as wide a consensus as possible, and on this basis to act as local agents of a world common good'. However, reining himself back in, Bull did concede that 'states are notoriously self-serving in their policies, and rightly suspected when they purport to act on behalf of the international community as a whole'.[116] Similarly, the posthumously published chapter 'The Importance of Grotius in the Study of International Relations' also includes hints that Bull was no longer as hostile towards the solidarist approach as he had been earlier in his career.[117] However, it is difficult to determine what these apparent shifts in Bull's thinking mean, in large part because he passed away before having the opportunity to account for them in more detail.

Conclusion

Despite the paucity of works that consider the influence of John Anderson on his student of international relations, Hedley Bull, the explication of Anderson's central ideas certainly takes us some way towards understanding many aspects of Bull's thought, particularly those that diverged most sharply from his more commonly acknowledged mentor, Martin Wight. Although similarities in Bull and Anderson's characters may be nothing more than a coincidence, it would be less plausible to suggest that Bull's emphasis on criticism as the basis of academic scholarship was not derived from a teacher who advocated this view so forcefully. Indeed, the centrality of the Socratic style to Bull's approach to both teaching and research, along with his penchant for somewhat brutal acts of demolition, render him an Andersonian of the highest order.

More significantly however, evident in both the teachings of Anderson and the works of Bull, is an inherent tension between conflict as a permanent feature of human society, and the mechanisms societies employ to mitigate its effects. In particular, both writers' discussions of social institutions constitute uneasy attempts to reconcile the apparently contradictory facts of human conflict and cooperation. Indeed, this tension apparent in Bull's works has been the subject of significant debate in contemporary international relations scholarship. Scholars have long debated the real extent of Bull's supposed 'realism', some seeking to reconcile his understanding of realism with his views on international society, whilst others have argued that he can more accurately be characterised as a rationalist, albeit an unself-conscious one. However, two aspects of Anderson's thought help to elucidate Bull's position. The first is derived from the empiricism of philosophical realism and is simply the view that whatever can be observed is as real as anything else that can be observed. Thus, the facts of conflict and cooperation in international relations are as real as each other. This would seem to suggest that there is no real need to reconcile these two contradictory observations. However, the second aspect of Anderson's thought that is of use here follows from the first and, adding the Heraclitean principles discussed above, maintains that institutions and cooperative social movements must be viewed in terms of the conflict they are designed to mitigate. Critically, such institutions are not normatively oriented but positively constructed to reflect actual, as opposed to desired, areas of agreement.

However, although Bull shared with Anderson a sceptical view of solidarism, religion and notions of common morality, he also deviated significantly from Anderson in this area. Indeed, for Bull, ethics remained central to the study of international relations, and became increasingly so as his career progressed. Perhaps this can be interpreted as a move away from Anderson as Bull's proximity to the influence of his teaching subsided, or perhaps it simply represents one of those shifts that active minds make over time. Either way, what is clear is that in many of his most forcefully defended ideas on religion and society, and in his critical style, Hedley Bull was of the same mould as his earliest mentor, the Socratic controversialist, John Anderson.

ENDNOTES

[1] I thank Ian Hall for providing substantial comments on several earlier drafts of this chapter. This chapter was first published as an article entitled 'Australian Realism and International Relations: John Anderson and Hedley Bull on Ethics, Religion and Society' in *International Politics*, vol. 45, 2008, pp. 52–71 and, with minor amendment, is reproduced here with the permission of the publisher, Palgrave Macmillan.

[2] The existence and membership of what is known as the 'English School' of international relations is a somewhat contentious issue in contemporary scholarship. For contending views on who ought to be considered a member of the 'school' and whether or not it ought to be considered a school at all see Tim Dunne, *Inventing International Society: A History of the English School*, Macmillan, London, 1998; Tim Dunne, 'All Along the Watchtower: A Reply to the Critics of Inventing International Society', *Conflict and Cooperation*, vol. 35, no. 2, 2001, pp. 227–38; Hidemi Suganami, 'A New Narrative, A New Subject? Tim Dunne on the English School', *Cooperation and Conflict*, vol. 35, no. 2, 2000, pp. 217–226; Hidemi Suganami, 'Heroes and a Villain: A Reply to Tim Dunne', *Cooperation and Conflict*, vol. 36, no. 3, 2001, pp. 327–30; Hidemi Suganami, 'British Institutionalists, or the English School, 20 Years On', *International Relations*, vol. 17, no. 3, September 2003, pp. 253–71; and Ian Hall, 'Still the English Patient? Closures and Inventions in the English School', *International Affairs*, vol. 77, no. 4, 2001, pp. 931–42. On this matter I am inclined to agree with Suganami's argument that 'it would be better to do away with the notion of the school altogether in this connection — because, however unintentionally, it tends to give the impression that a clear boundary could, or should, be found between those who are in and those who are out' (Hidemi Suganami, 'C.A.W. Manning and the Study of International Relations', *Review of International Studies*, vol. 27, 2001, pp. 91–107 (100)).

[3] Tim Dunne, *Inventing International Society: A History of the English School*, Macmillan, London, p. 136.

[4] Hedley Bull, 'Martin Wight and the Theory of International Relations', in Gabriele Wight and Brian Porter (eds), *International Theory: The Three Traditions*, Leicester University Press, London, 1991, pp. ix–xxiii (ix).

[5] Hedley Bull, *The Anarchical Society: A Study of Order in World Politics*, 2nd edn., Macmillan, London, 1995, p. xiii.

[6] João .Marques de Almeida, 'Challenging Realism by Returning to History: The British Committee's Contribution to International Relations 40 Years On', *International Relations*, vol. 17, no. 3, 2003, pp. 273–303 (p. 292).

[7] John Donald Bruce Miller, 'Hedley Bull, 1932–1985', in J.D.B. Miller and R.J. Vincent (eds), *Order and Violence: Hedley Bull and International Relations*, Clarendon Press, Oxford, 1990, p. 3; and Suganami, 'C.A.W. Manning and the Study of International Relations', *Review of International Studies*, pp. 91–107 (95).

[8] Among those who do mention Anderson's influence on Bull are Miller, 'Hedley Bull, 1932–1985', in J.D.B. Miller and R.J. Vincent (eds), *Order and Violence: Hedley Bull and International Relations*, Clarendon, pp. 2–3; J.L. Richardson, 'The Academic Study of International Relations', in J.D.B. Miller and R.J. Vincent (eds), *Order and Violence: Hedley Bull and International Relations*, Clarendon Press, Oxford, 1990, pp. 175–77; and Robert O'Neill and David N. Schwartz (eds), *Hedley Bull on Arms Control*, Macmillan, London, 1987, pp. 2–3.

[9] Bull, *The Anarchical Society: A Study of Order in World Politics*, p. xiv.

[10] David M. Armstrong, 'Introduction', to University of Sydney, *Australian Studies Resources, Professor John Anderson 1893–1962*, John Anderson Lecture Notes and Other Writings, available at <http://setis.library.usyd.edu.au/anderson/>, accessed 25 June 2008.

[11] John Passmore, 'Anderson as a Systematic Philosopher', *Quadrant*, vol. 21, 1977, pp. 48–53 (53).

[12] John Anderson, *Education and Politics*, Angus and Robertson, Sydney, 1931; John Anderson, 'Classicalism', in *Studies in Empirical Philosophy*, 2nd edition, Angus and Robertson, Sydney, 1962; John Anderson, in D.Z. Phillips (ed.) *Education and Inquiry*, Blackwell, Oxford, 1980; John Anderson, in J. Anderson, G. Cullum and K. Lycos (eds), *Art and Reality*, Hale and Iremonger, Sydney, 1982; and University of Sydney, *Australian Studies Resources, Professor John Anderson 1893–1962*, John Anderson Lecture Notes and Other Writings, available at <http://setis.library.usyd.edu.au/anderson/>, accessed 25 June 2008.

[13] Jim Baker, *Australian Realism: The Systematic Philosophy of John Anderson*, Cambridge University Press, Cambridge, 1986, pp. 10–11.

[14] John Anderson, 'Literary Censorship', *Honi Soit*, 16 July 1930.

[15] David Stove, 'The Force of Intellect: Fifty Years of John Anderson', *Quadrant*, vol. 21, 1977, pp. 45–46 (45). For more comprehensive biographical treatments of Anderson see Armstrong, 'Introduction', to University of Sydney, *Australian Studies Resources, Professor John Anderson 1893–1962*, John Anderson Lecture Notes and Other Writings, available at <http://setis.library.usyd.edu.au/anderson/>, accessed 25 June 2008; Jim Baker (ed.), *Australian Realism: The Systematic Philosophy of John Anderson*; James Franklin, *Corrupting the Youth: A History of Philosophy in Australia*, Macleay Press, Paddington, 2003; S.A. Grave, *The History of Philosophy in Australia*, University of Queensland Press, Brisbane, 1984; John A. Passmore, *Memoirs of a Semi-Detached Australian*, Melbourne University Press, Carlton, 1997; Anthony Quinton, 'Introduction', in Jim Baker (ed.), *Australian Realism: The Systematic Philosophy of John Anderson*; and M. Weblin, 'Background Notes', to University of Sydney, *Australian Studies Resources, Professor John Anderson 1893–1962*, John Anderson Lecture Notes and Other Writings, available at <http://setis.library.usyd.edu.au/anderson/>, accessed 25 June 2008.

[16] In a report of his 1941 address to the Freethought Society titled 'Christianity, Faith and Credulity', John Anderson is described as the 'local Socrates'. (See John Anderson, 'Christianity, Faith and Credulity', University of Sydney, *Australian Studies Resources, Professor John Anderson 1893–1962*, John Anderson Lecture Notes and Other Writings, available at <http://setis.library.usyd.edu.au/anderson/>, accessed 25 June 2008.)

[17] Peter Shrubb in *The Bulletin*, 30 June 1962.

[18] John Anderson, 'The Place of the Academic in Modern Society', in D.Z. Phillips (ed.), *Education and Inquiry*, Blackwell, Oxford, 1980, p. 214.

[19] Passmore, *Memoirs of a Semi-Detached Australian*, p. 94.

[20] Passmore, *Memoirs of a Semi-Detached Australian*, p. 94.

[21] Stove, 'The Force of Intellect: Fifty Years of John Anderson', *Quadrant*, vol. 21, 1977, pp. 45–46 (45).

[22] John Anderson in Franklin, *Corrupting the Youth: A History of Philosophy in Australia*, p. 22.

[23] David M. Armstrong in R.J. Bogdan (ed.), in *D.M. Armstrong*, Reidel, Dordrecht and Boston, 1984, p. 7.

[24] David M. Armstrong in Franklin, *Corrupting the Youth: A History of Philosophy in Australia*, p. 47.

[25] Passmore, *Memoirs of a Semi-Detached Australian*, p. 93.

[26] Armstrong, 'Introduction', to University of Sydney, *Australian Studies Resources, Professor John Anderson 1893–1962*, John Anderson Lecture Notes and Other Writings, available at <http://setis.library.usyd.edu.au/anderson/>, accessed 25 June 2008.

[27] John Anderson, 'Realism and Some of its Critics', in *Studies in Empirical Philosophy*, 1930, available at <http://setis.library.usyd.edu.au/anderson/>, accessed 25 June 2008.

[28] Grave, *The History of Philosophy in Australia*, p. 31.

[29] Passmore, 'John Anderson and twentieth century philosophy', 2001, p. x, available at <http://setis.library.usyd.edu.au/anderson/>, accessed 25 June 2008, p. ix.

[30] Grave, *The History of Philosophy in Australia*, p. 24. The first person to hold that Challis Chair, Francis Anderson, had been Caird's assistant in Glasgow and, although not as fervent an exponent of idealist philosophy as Caird, was an idealist nonetheless.

[31] Baker, *Australian Realism: The Systematic Philosophy of John Anderson*, pp. 3–4.

[32] Baker, *Australian Realism: The Systematic Philosophy of John Anderson*, p. 4.

[33] Grave, *The History of Philosophy in Australia*, p. 37.

[34] Quinton, 'Introduction', in Jim Baker (ed.), *Australian Realism: The Systematic Philosophy of John Anderson*, p. x, 1986.

[35] Bull, *The Anarchical Society: A Study of Order in World Politics*, p. xiii.

[36] John Anderson, 'Realism', *Writings of John Anderson: Miscellaneous Philosophical Writings 1927–1958*, 1958, available at <http://setis.library.usyd.edu.au/anderson/>, accessed 25 June 2008.

[37] M. Weblin, 'Introduction' to John Anderson, *Space-time and the Proposition: The 1944 Lectures on Samuel Alexander's Space, Time and Diety*, Sydney University Press, Sydney, 2005, p. 84

[38] Anderson, 'Realism and Some of its Critics', in *Studies in Empirical Philosophy*, 1930, available at <http://setis.library.usyd.edu.au/anderson/>, accessed 25 June 2008, p. 4.

[39] John Anderson, 'Empiricism', in *John Anderson: Studies in Empirical Philosophy*, 1927, available at <http://setis.library.usyd.edu.au/anderson/>, accessed 25 June 2008, p. 1.

[40] Quinton, 'Introduction', in Jim Baker (ed.) *Australian Realism: The Systematic Philosophy of John Anderson*, pp. xii–xiii.

[41] Anderson, 'Realism and Some of its Critics', in *Studies in Empirical Philosophy*, 1930, available at <http://setis.library.usyd.edu.au/anderson/>, accessed 25 June 2008, p. 24.

[42] Baker, *Australian Realism: The Systematic Philosophy of John Anderson*, p. 1.

[43] Passmore, 'John Anderson and twentieth century philosophy', 2001, p. x, available at <http://setis.library.usyd.edu.au/anderson/>, accessed 25 June 2008.

[44] Anderson, 'Empiricism', in *John Anderson: Studies in Empirical Philosophy*, 1927, available at <http://setis.library.usyd.edu.au/anderson/>, accessed 25 June 2008, p. 1.

[45] Baker, *Australian Realism: The Systematic Philosophy of John Anderson*, p. 34.

[46] Passmore, 'John Anderson and twentieth century philosophy', 2001, p. xi, available at <http://setis.library.usyd.edu.au/anderson/>, accessed 25 June 2008.

[47] Baker, *Australian Realism: The Systematic Philosophy of John Anderson*, p. 34.

[48] Anderson, 'Realism and Some of its Critics', in *Studies in Empirical Philosophy*, 1930, available at <http://setis.library.usyd.edu.au/anderson/>, accessed 25 June 2008, p. 39.

[49] Baker, *Australian Realism: The Systematic Philosophy of John Anderson*, p. 121.

[50] Passmore, 'John Anderson and twentieth century philosophy', 2001, p. xix, available at <http://setis.library.usyd.edu.au/anderson/>, accessed 25 June 2008.

[51] John Anderson, 'The Nature of Ethics', in *Studies in Empirical Philosophy*, 1943, available at <http://setis.library.usyd.edu.au/anderson/>, accessed 25 June 2008, p. 1.

[52] John Anderson, 'Realism vs Relativism in Ethics', in *Studies in Empirical Philosophy*, 1933, available at <http://setis.library.usyd.edu.au/anderson/>, accessed 25 June 2008, p. 4.

[53] As the founder of the Freethought Society at the University of Sydney, the notion of freethought was central to Anderson's approach.

[54] John Anderson, 'The Nature of Freethought' (1950), *Writings of John Anderson: The Bronze Age 1946–1951*, available at <http://setis.library.usyd.edu.au/anderson/>, accessed 25 June 2008.

[55] John Anderson, 'Determinism and Ethics', in *Studies in Empirical Philosophy*, 1928, available at <http://setis.library.usyd.edu.au/anderson/>, accessed 25 June 2008, p. 2.

[56] Anderson, 'Determinism and Ethics', in *Studies in Empirical Philosophy*, 1928, available at <http://setis.library.usyd.edu.au/anderson/>, accessed 25 June 2008, p. 3.

[57] Anderson, 'Determinism and Ethics', in *Studies in Empirical Philosophy*, 1928, available at <http://setis.library.usyd.edu.au/anderson/>, accessed 25 June 2008, p. 29.

[58] Quinton, 'Introduction', in Jim Baker (ed.), *Australian Realism: The Systematic Philosophy of John Anderson*, pp. xvi.

[59] Baker, *Australian Realism: The Systematic Philosophy of John Anderson*, p. 116.

[60] John Anderson, 'Religion in Education' (1943), *Writings of John Anderson: The Silver Age 1938–1945*, available at <http://setis.library.usyd.edu.au/anderson/>, accessed 25 June 2008.

[61] John Anderson, 'Ethics and Religion', 1955, available at <http://setis.library.usyd.edu.au/anderson/>, accessed 25 June 2008.

[62] Weblin, 'Background Notes', to University of Sydney, *Australian Studies Resources, Professor John Anderson 1893–1962*, John Anderson Lecture Notes and Other Writings, <http://setis.library.usyd.edu.au/anderson/>, accessed 25 June 2008.

[63] John Anderson, 'Philosophy and Religion', Lecture I, 003/031/1954, University of Sydney Archives, 1954, available at <http://setis.library.usyd.edu.au/oztexts/lectures.html>, accessed 10 September 2005, p. I.

[64] Anderson, 'Religion in Education' (1943), *Writings of John Anderson: The Silver Age 1938–1945*, available at <http://setis.library.usyd.edu.au/anderson/>, accessed 25 June 2008.

[65] Pam Stavropoulos, 'Conservative Radical: the Conservatism of John Anderson', *Australian Journal of Anthropology*, vol. 3, nos. 1 & 2, 1992, pp. 67–79 (73).

[66] Baker, *Australian Realism: The Systematic Philosophy of John Anderson*, p. 127.

[67] Baker, *Australian Realism: The Systematic Philosophy of John Anderson*, p. 127.

[68] Baker, *Australian Realism: The Systematic Philosophy of John Anderson*, p. 127.

[69] I.F. Helu, 'Anderson, Heraclitus and Social Science', *Australian Journal of Anthropology*, vol. 3, nos. 1 & 2, 1992, pp. 22–31 (24).

[70] Helu, 'Anderson, Heraclitus and Social Science', *Australian Journal of Anthropology*, pp. 22–31 (23-24).

[71] Heraclitus (DK22B80), quoted in Helu, 'Anderson. Heraclitus and Social Science', p. 24.

[72] Anderson, 'Classicalism', in *Studies in Empirical Philosophy*, p. 194.

[73] Brian Kennedy, 'John Anderson and Marxism', *Australian Journal of Anthropology*, vol. 3, nos. 1 & 2, 1992, pp. 55–66 (61).

[74] Kennedy, 'John Anderson and Marxism', *Australian Journal of Anthropology*, pp. 55–66 (64)

[75] Weblin, 'Background Notes', to University of Sydney, *Australian Studies Resources, Professor John Anderson 1893–1962*, John Anderson Lecture Notes and Other Writings, <http://setis.library.usyd.edu.au/anderson/>, accessed 25 June 2008.

[76] John Arthur Passmore, *Philosophical Reasoning*, Scribner, New York, 1962, p. xxii.

[77] Helu, 'Anderson, Heraclitus and Social Science', *Australian Journal of Anthropology*, pp. 22–31 (25).

[78] Ian Hall, 'Challenge and Response: The Lasting Engagement of Arnold J. Toynbee and Martin Wight', *International Relations*, vol. 17, no. 3, 2003, pp. 389–404 (393). For a more detailed consideration of Wight's religious views see I. Hall, *The International Thought of Martin Wight*, Palgrave Macmillan, New York, 2006 (chapter 2).

[79] Bull, 'Martin Wight and the Theory of International Relations', in G. Wight and B. Porter (eds), *International Theory: The Three Traditions*, pp. ix–xxiii (xxiii).

[80] Michael Howard, 'Hedley Norman Bull', *Proceedings of the British Academy*, vol. 72, 1986, pp. 395–408 (395).

[81] Michael Howard, 'Hedley Bull: A Eulogy for his Memorial Service', in R. O'Neill and D.N. Schwartz (eds), *Hedley Bull on Arms Control*, p. 276.

[82] Richardson, 'The Academic Study of International Relations', in J.D.B. Miller and R.J. Vincent (eds), *Order and Violence: Hedley Bull and International Relations*, pp. 145–77 (pp. 149 and 175).

[83] Don Markwell, 'Hedley Bull as a Teacher', in R. O'Neill and D.N. Schwartz (eds), *Hedley Bull on Arms Control*, p. 280.

[84] Miller, 'Hedley Bull, 1932–1985', in J.D.B. Miller and R.J. Vincent (eds), *Order and Violence: Hedley Bull and International Relations*, p. 10.

[85] Hedley Bull, 'The Theory of International Politics, 1919–1969', in B. Porter (ed.), *The Aberystwyth Papers: International Politics 1919–1969*, Oxford University Press, London, 1972, p. 32.

[86] Miller, 'Hedley Bull, 1932–1985', in J.D.B. Miller and R.J. Vincent (eds), *Order and Violence: Hedley Bull and International Relations*, p. 10.

[87] Markwell, 'Hedley Bull as a Teacher', in R. O'Neill and D.N. Schwartz (eds), *Hedley Bull on Arms Control*, p. 279.

[88] O'Neill and Schwartz, *Hedley Bull on Arms Control*, p. 3.

[89] Hedley Bull, 'International Theory: The Case for a Classical Approach', *World Politics*, vol. 18, no. 3, 1966, pp. 361–77 (362).

[90] Bull, 'International Theory: The Case for a Classical Approach', *World Politics*, pp. 361–77 (370).

[91] Bull, 'International Theory: The Case for a Classical Approach', *World Politics*, pp. 361–77 (370).

[92] Bull, 'International Theory: The Case for a Classical Approach', *World Politics*, pp. 361–77 (371).

[93] Maurice Keens-Soper, 'Letters from Maurice Keens-Soper to Martin Wight', Wight MSS 233 6/9, 9 August 1971.

[94] Bull, *The Anarchical Society: A Study of Order in World Politics*, p. 13.

[95] Stanley Hoffman, 'International Society', in J.D.B. Miller and R.J. Vincent (eds), *Order and Violence: Hedley Bull and International Relations*, Clarendon Press, Oxford, 1990, pp. 13–37 (24).

[96] Hedley Bull, 'The Grotian Conception of International Society', in H. Butterfield and M. Wight (eds), *Diplomatic Investigations: Essays on the Theory of International Politics*, George Allen & Unwin, London, 1966, pp. 71–72.

[97] de Almeida, 'Challenging Realism by Returning to History: The British Committee's Contribution to International Relations 40 Years On', pp. 292–93.

[98] Bull, 'The Grotian Conception of International Society', in H. Butterfield and M. Wight (eds), *Diplomatic Investigations: Essays on the Theory of International Politics*, p. 68.

[99] Bull, *The Anarchical Society: A Study of Order in World Politics*, p. 230.

[100] Bull, 'The Grotian Conception of International Society', in Butterfield and Wight (eds), *Diplomatic Investigations: Essays on the Theory of International Politics*, p. 70.

[101] Suganami also notes the possible influence of Manning on Bull's pluralism and critique of solidarism (Suganami, 'C.A.W. Manning and the Study of International Relations', *Review of International Studies*, pp. 91–107 (95)).

[102] O'Neill and Schwartz, *Hedley Bull on Arms Control*, pp. 2–3.

[103] Stanley Hoffman, 'International Society', in J.D.B. Miller and R.J. Vincent (eds), *Order and Violence: Hedley Bull and International Relations*, pp. 13–37 (21).

[104] E.B.F. Midgley, *The Natural Law Tradition and the Theory of International Relations*, Harper & Row, New York, 1975.

[105] Hedley Bull, 'Natural Law and International Relations', *British Journal of International Studies*, vol. 5, 1979, pp. 171–81 (171).

[106] Bull, 'Natural Law and International Relations', pp. 171–81 (181).

[107] Bull, 'Natural Law and International Relations', pp. 171–81 (179).

[108] Bull, 'Natural Law and International Relations', pp. 171–81 (180).

[109] Hedley Bull, 'Recapturing the Just War for Political Theory', *World Politics*, vol. 31, no. 4, 1979, pp. 588–99 (591)

[110] Bull, 'Recapturing the Just War for Political Theory', pp. 588–99 (597).

[111] Bull, 'Recapturing the Just War for Political Theory', pp. 588–99 (596).

[112] Bull, 'Recapturing the Just War for Political Theory', pp. 588–99 (597).

[113] Nicholas J. Wheeler and Timothy Dunne, 'Hedley Bull's Pluralism of the Intellect and Solidarism of the Will', *International Affairs*, vol. 72, no. 1, 1996, pp. 91–107.

[114] Wheeler and Dunne, 'Hedley Bull's Pluralism of the Intellect and Solidarism of the Will', p. 96.

[115] Hedley Bull in Wheeler and Dunne, 'Hedley Bull's Pluralism of the Intellect and Solidarism of the Will', p. 99.

[116] Hedley Bull, *Justice in International Relations*, The Hagey Lectures, University of Waterloo, Waterloo, 1984, p. 14.

[117] Hedley Bull, 'The Importance of Grotius in the Study of International Relations', in H. Bull, B. Kingsbury and A. Roberts (eds), *Hugo Grotius and International Relations*, Clarendon Press, Oxford, 1990, pp. 65–94.

Chapter 3

Hedley Bull and Arms Control

Robert O'Neill

A New Field

The challenging and sensitive field of arms control proved to be Hedley Bull's route to international prominence. In the mid-1950s many people who had the knowledge to think about nuclear weapons believed that the world was heading for danger. Nuclear warheads were growing rapidly in numbers and explosive power. New types of nuclear systems were proliferating, from air-dropped bombs to ballistic missiles. Submarine-launched missiles were also under development. Although the nuclear arsenal of the United States was large, that of the Soviet Union was promising to burgeon. This trend, plus the higher degree of secrecy that the Soviets could maintain, encouraged some influential Westerners to take the pessimistic view that unless the United States pressed ahead with a much stronger rearmament program, it would find itself outclassed by Soviet throw weight. The missile-gap controversy was beginning to open up. And the proliferation issue was already emerging. Britain had its own tested and proved nuclear weapons, France was known to be developing them, China (the United States' main opponent in the recently halted Korean War) was another clear possibility, and then there were several other advanced states such as Italy, the Federal Republic of Germany and Sweden (not to mention Australia) which could credibly attempt to build their own nuclear weapons.

Perhaps even more important than the vertical proliferation issues (size and types of weapons held by a single power) and the horizontal proliferation issues (numbers of states with their own nuclear weapons) was the basic question: 'What rational purpose did nuclear weapons serve?' By the mid-1950s these three sets of issues were becoming matters for public discussion and policy debate in the West. Leading politicians, academics, journalists, churchmen, retired armed service officers and diplomats were airing their thoughts in the newspapers, on radio, through public meetings and forums, and even via the relatively new medium of television. Any major set of problems which had the potential to threaten the security of whole nations and alliance systems was bound to attract the interest of major philanthropic foundations in the United States and Western Europe. Those who were seriously interested in these problems could now hope to obtain significant financial backing for undertaking major research and analytical projects in the field of nuclear weapons policy. Their results would pass immediately into the public domain. Because this was a relatively new field, one in which there were few practitioners to dominate the discussion, newcomers could achieve prominence in a way that they could not in, for example, the fields of major naval warfare, or tank strategy. Bold individuals and groups of concerned, but not yet necessarily very expert, investigators could compete for foundation funding and then, once winning a grant, they could move ahead with attempting to develop better policies in the field of nuclear weapons.

A New Investigator

One of these individuals was Philip Noel-Baker, a former minister in the Attlee Government who was deeply committed to the cause of disarmament and had achieved international prominence through his writings on the subject during the 1920s and 1930s. Noel-Baker was a Quaker with a distinguished record of ambulance service during the First World War, a former Olympic athlete (Captain of the British track team at the 1924 Olympic Games in Paris which was the subject of the 1981 film *Chariots of Fire*) and a former holder of the Sir Ernest Cassell Chair in International Law at the University of London. He was committed to an ambitious task in the 1950s: the production of a book on the arms race and how it might be checked. He also had plans for a further book on the major disarmament conferences sponsored by the League of Nations in the inter-war years. Noel-Baker recognised that he needed assistance with a project of this magnitude and looked around for a young scholar whom he could respect and whose wits matched his own. He was guided to a newly appointed Assistant Lecturer in International Relations at the London School of Economics, the recent Oxford graduate Hedley Bull, and a working partnership was formed in 1956, the year in which the Olympic Games were held in Australia.

His First Task

Despite Noel-Baker's impressive record as a thinker, scholar and politician, the young scholar from Sydney was sceptical about the feasibility of his senior colleague's grand design for general and complete disarmament. Bull's first task, probably for Noel-Baker's next project rather than the volume he published in 1958, *The Arms Race: A Programme for World Disarmament*, was to go through the records of the disarmament conferences of the 1930s to see if they had been successful in narrowing differences to the extent that there was some prospect of a significant agreement. Bull soon saw that the differences between the major states remained wide, and they increased as international tensions grew in East Asia and in Central Europe. There was no real prospect of success by moving along that path. If disarmament were to come at all (as Bull hoped it might but in lasting form), it would be limited in its scope and would endure only where mutual advantage between negotiating partners was realised. Bull questioned the feasibility of the whole international community agreeing suddenly to dispense with all means of defending national sovereignty, national interests or even of administering a sharp lesson to an annoying neighbour. Noel-Baker and Bull parted company in 1957. Although the partnership had not been fruitful, the experience had aroused Bull's interest in the problems of disarmament and he was soon to have the opportunity to develop his own line of thinking for an influential and appreciative audience.

Ironically Hedley was nearly claimed by the arms race of the Cold War itself. In 1957 he received call-up papers from the British Government for national service. All Commonwealth citizens below the age of 26, living in and paying taxes to the United Kingdom, were eligible at that time for British military service. Hedley thought briefly that he might actually have to don a uniform and be trained by the British Army, a prospect that he did not altogether shun. However his head of department at the London School of Economics (LSE), Charles Manning, was horrified at the prospect of losing Bull for two years, not to mention being apprehensive at the degree of risk to which Hedley might be subjected personally during his period of service. Manning used his extensive network of contacts to see that Bull was elected to a Rockefeller fellowship for 1957–58 which would take him out of the United Kingdom for the crucial period until he had passed his 26th birthday.

This was a very fortunate move from Hedley's perspective, enabling him and his wife Mary to spend nearly 12 months among leading scholars in the field of Strategic Studies in the United States before returning to the United Kingdom via Australia, re-uniting with families and friends. He went first to the Center for International Affairs at Harvard, directed then by Robert Bowie. He also had ample opportunity for interchange of ideas with other Harvard scholars such as Tom Schelling and Henry Kissinger. He visited Herman Kahn at the Hudson Institute, who was developing the central ideas in his celebrated book *Thinking about the Unthinkable*, a volume which dealt with the consequences of the actual use of nuclear weapons in war. Bull was in strong disagreement with many of Kahn's views, but admired the rigour of the research which went into the production of his publications.

In the New Year Hedley and Mary moved on to spend six weeks at the Johns Hopkins School of Advanced International Studies in Washington, DC where Hedley came to know several other leaders in the field such as Paul Nitze and Robert Osgood. Their next stay was for four months at the University of Chicago, where Hedley had lively discussions with Morton Kaplan. At the end of May they drove to San Francisco, via Yellowstone National Park, for a few weeks at the University of California, Berkeley before crossing the Pacific to Sydney in July 1958. After a few weeks with family and friends, they embarked once more for Britain. Hedley found on his return to London that, as a result of his travels and the quality of the people he had formed links with, he was regarded as the person who knew most about the American scene in international security among London academics. This cachet made him particularly interesting to the Director of the recently established Institute for Strategic Studies (ISS), Alastair Buchan. Bull naturally was keen to take part in Institute activities and he found a ready reception.

The ISS (to be known as the IISS once it had added the word 'International' to its title in 1964) had been founded by a group of British scholars, journalists, churchmen, former civil servants, diplomats and armed service officers known as the Brighton Conference Association. They had come together at Brighton in January 1957 to grapple with the question of whether nuclear weapons served a rational purpose and if so, how they might be incorporated into Western strategic doctrine without counter-productive effect. The group had played a useful part in helping Noel-Baker with his book. By late 1958 this group had sufficient funds and sense of purpose to establish the new Institute and to attract Buchan to be its executive head. In 1958–59 Buchan came to know Bull well and was very favourably impressed by his capacity to argue forcefully, his knowledge of international history, and his very pragmatic approach to the issues of what would and what would not gain political support in the international arena.

In the meantime Noel-Baker had achieved a great impact with his publication of *The Arms Race* in the same year. The book had a strong appeal to many on the liberal and socialist sides of politics, to those who saw the Second World War as having been caused by the League of Nations having too little power and authority rather than too much, and to those who saw nuclear weapons in particular as a means of dominating international affairs. In 1959 Noel-Baker was awarded the Nobel Prize for Peace and his influence in his own circle was strengthened thereby. In 1961 he won the Schweitzer Prize for *The Arms Race*.

Hedley Bull, far from being intimidated by this acclamation for what he regarded as a seriously flawed work, saw it as all the more reason for mounting a strong attack on Noel-Baker's ideas. In 1959 he published a long review of *The Arms Race* in *The Australian Journal of Politics and History* which, while paying Noel-Baker proper respect for his distinguished career, was strongly critical of his current line of thinking.[1]

Initial Exposition of His Ideas

Bull used this opportunity to lay out his thinking on the role that disarmament could play in securing peace more adequately than it had in the past. He was Clausewitzian in his approach, arguing that wars were caused by political tensions rather than the mere accumulation of arms. Hence peace had to be sought more through political agreement and understanding than disarmament. He was opposed to the development of any one central world authority, as some (including Noel-Baker) were arguing that the United Nations should become. Bull feared that such a body would be too powerful and oppressive. He preferred a diversity of centres of power which might lead to friction and wars from time to time, but one which also enabled freedom and individuality to survive in the international community.

He also dismissed the notion that states would substantially disarm by mutual agreement, as most governments and their electorates believed that they needed weapons for the defence of their liberty or to hit back at others who seriously infringed their freedom of action. Where disarmament had some real prospects, Bull argued, was in the field of limited scope agreements, presciently pointing the way to the limited, strictly defined arms control agreements of the 1960s, 1970s and 1980s such as SALT I and II, the Partial Test Ban Treaty, the ABM Treaty and the Nuclear Non-Proliferation Treaty itself. This latter treaty, through attempting of necessity to be universal in its membership, did not fulfil Bull's criteria for success as fully as the others. Unsurprisingly it has remained weaker in its effect and has been defied by notable proliferating powers. It has also been frustrated, as many have argued including Bull, by the tardiness of the five declared and accepted nuclear weapon states to reduce their own nuclear arsenals.

Bull made a distinction between nuclear weapons intended for deterrence and those intended for use in combat. He accepted the need for weapons to serve the first purpose, invalidating Noel-Baker's claim that 'if war is an anachronism then armaments are too'. It was the very frightfulness of nuclear weapons that made war anachronistic. They had a continuing and positive role to play—to make war less frightful would be to make it more probable Bull argued. Bull however refused to accept that nuclear weapons should be developed as a means of combat. Their effect would be too horrible, and the use of low yield nuclear weapons in the early stages of a conflict was likely to encourage others to escalate their usage of them, resulting in a holocaust. To that extent, Bull shared Noel-Baker's view of nuclear weapons. He recognised them as a formidable problem for statesmen and diplomats to deal with, and for defence ministries and armed services to keep tightly under control, but in the context of the world order then extant in the 1950s Bull thought that the objectives of the nuclear abolitionists such as the Campaign for Nuclear Disarmament were futile.

Bull came quite early to believe that it would be morally wrong and militarily counter-productive to be the first to use nuclear weapons, particularly in a conflict between the North Atlantic Treaty Organization (NATO) and the Warsaw Pact. He joined those who advocated a 'No First Use' agreement between both sides and put himself into a position of lasting difference with United States and NATO policymakers. Western leaders, looking at the unfavourable balance of their conventional forces with those of the Warsaw Pact, believed that a credible threat to use nuclear weapons first in reply to any Soviet use of massive force in Europe or elsewhere was a vital part of deterrence. And the fact that the Soviets continued to advocate such a 'No First Use' agreement made it seem only less desirable from a NATO perspective. Bull did not constantly harp on the matter, but he regularly drew fire from NATO-member officials such as Sir Michael Quinlan when he expressed his viewpoint in international conferences.

The logic of his stance on nuclear weapons as disincentives to war led Bull to oppose the idea of strategic defence against an enemy's nuclear weapons. He was explicit on this point in his review article of 1959 and he kept to these views, especially during the heated debates of the 1970s and 1980s on programs such as US President Ronald Reagan's Strategic Defence Initiative (SDI).

Working with the Institute for Strategic Studies

Thus by 1959 Bull had set forth his views on the desirability and scope of arms limitation agreements in the nuclear era, and his thoughts achieved resonance among specialists in Western Europe and North America. They were particularly interesting to Alastair Buchan, who was putting together a team of leading analysts to make a major attempt to develop more rational Western policies on the roles and use of nuclear weapons in order to minimise their dangers. A key person in any such team, of course, is the rapporteur or author of the final report, and Buchan saw in Bull the ideal person for this important job. It was vital to the newly founded ISS for its product to be regarded as of the highest quality. As the project progressed in 1959–60, the senior members of the team, including Michael Howard and Richard Goold-Adams, became increasingly impressed by the presentations that Bull made at discussion meetings and they encouraged him to expand and deepen his efforts. The group met every few weeks to hear and discuss a paper prepared by Bull. The group's enthusiasm mounted. Participants could see not only that in each of these papers they had close to a chapter for the resulting book, but also that they could be confident that the book would achieve a major impact.

In 1960 the ISS held its second annual conference, at Oxford, on the theme of arms control. Bull was appointed rapporteur for the conference. The rapporteur was not just a reporter of the proceedings, but was given a full plenary session at the conclusion of proceedings both to sum up what the conference had achieved and to give his own thoughts on the main topics under discussion. As Michael Howard, one of the conference participants, has recorded in his memoirs:

> The text he [Bull] provided for discussion, later published under the title *The Control of the Arms Race*, was to become a classic. Hedley was an abrasive young Australian who had no time for the woolly cant that well-meaning liberals had accumulated around the topic over the past half-century, and to watch him deftly despatch their sacred cows was a

sheer joy. We could not reinvent the world he argued: we live inevitably in a world of mistrustful sovereign powers, and the best we could do was to make it possible for them to distrust one another a little less. It would not be too much to say that his little book revolutionised thinking on the subject. It should still be the point of departure for both academics and bureaucrats.[2]

Fortified no doubt by his reception from some of the North Atlantic community's leading thinkers in this field, Bull handed the manuscript to Buchan and the ISS published it in 1961 under the title *The Control of the Arms Race*. It was the Institute's second book in a long and distinguished series titled *Studies in International Security*. As Michael Howard has said, this volume established him as the leading newcomer in the field of nuclear arms control policy. It also helped to publicise the idea of arms control rather than disarmament, moving the policy debate into a much more fruitful course. In the following year Bull was promoted to be a Reader in International Relations at the LSE. His book appeared just after the Kennedy Administration had been elected to office in the United States. The incoming US Government was very interested in arms control and Bull received a wide readership on both sides of the Atlantic.

An Interval of Government Service

When Harold Wilson and the Labour Party won the British elections in 1964, the new government, at the urgings of the Party Conference, and no doubt with some impetus from Noel-Baker who remained an Member of Parliament and had become chairman of the Parliamentary Foreign Affairs Group of Labour MPs, decided to establish a branch of the Foreign Office specifically devoted to disarmament. The government then had to find a capable and not too ideological a person to be the minister responsible for this new activity. After looking at several, Wilson's choice finally rested on Alun Gwynne-Jones, a former army officer who had became the defence correspondent of *The Times* in 1961. Gwynne-Jones was appointed Lord Chalfont, enabling him to sit in the House of Lords. He was also a member of the ISS and knew of Bull's formidable expertise in his intended field. Chalfont recognised that he needed expert assistance in his new field and enlisted Hedley Bull to be the first Director of the Arms Control and Disarmament Research Unit at the Foreign Office. Bull received two years leave of absence from the LSE and took up his new duties at the beginning of 1965.

This appointment required Bull to have access to papers which had been classified as 'for UK eyes only', a way of keeping them private from the Americans among others. Bull had already been thinking about taking British nationality to make international travel in Europe easier than with an Australian passport. He thought by taking this step he would facilitate his access in the Foreign

Office, but what he did not know was that the Australian Government did not recognise dual nationality (except for British nationals taking up Australian citizenship), and that by taking British nationality he would lose his Australian citizenship. This was a serious matter for him but by the time he found out about it, too much water had flowed under the bridge. Bull became the holder of a British passport, which he then retained for the rest of his life despite a period of ten years in Australia (1967–77) when he was a Professor of International Relations at The Australian National University in Canberra.

Bull inevitably got into scrapes with the formal bureaucratic procedures of the Foreign Office. Believing that many papers were given security classifications way beyond what the material they contained justified, he was not above opening his briefcase while on a bus or the underground and pulling out a file conspicuously marked 'SECRET'. On at least one of these occasions someone with high official access caught Bull in this infringement of security rules and reported him to the Foreign Office. Bull was duly carpeted and had to agree to mend his ways.

While Bull found the work of the Arms Control and Disarmament Research Unit interesting, he, unsurprisingly, did not take to bureaucratic life. He saw that he was too junior and too much of an outsider to be able ever to have a major influence on British Government policies on nuclear weapons. Therefore he did not delude himself that he had made a permanent change in his profession and working environment. Nonetheless, building the Unit gave him a chance to identify and bring in experts such as Geoff Jukes, Jim Richardson (another Australian) and Ian Bellany (all three of whom were subsequently to hold posts at The Australian National University). The post also gave him opportunities for dialogue with important foreign specialists in this field, especially in the United States. The Unit gave valuable support to the British delegation to the Geneva arms control negotiations, especially on non-proliferation matters in the years while the Nuclear Non-Proliferation Treaty was being put together. Bull's interest in strategic defences, especially his concern that they might make nuclear weapons more usable rather than less, led him to follow this issue closely in his contacts with the Kennedy and Johnson Administrations, long before the Strategic Defence Initiative was announced by Reagan.

His Return to Australia

By 1967 Bull faced a serious decision. Either he returned to the LSE or he became a long-term professional member of the Foreign Office. Fortunately his dilemma was resolved by a very welcome invitation from Australia. Bruce Miller, the Head of the Department of International Relations in the Research School of Pacific Studies at The Australian National University, Canberra, had been able to open the way for a second full professorship to be established there, with Hedley Bull in mind as the person who should hold it. In the way of these things it was a short-lived opportunity and Bull had to make up his mind quickly before the vagaries of University politics allowed another department to claim the necessary funds. Once he had taken the decision to accept and move back to Australia all went well with the appointment process and Bull was soon in Canberra, which was to be his base for the next decade.

Although I had met Hedley while I was a graduate student at Oxford in the early 1960s our paths did not overlap until he returned to Australia, by which time I had completed my studies at Oxford and served for a year as an infantry officer in the Vietnam War. I remember expressing some surprise to him that he had given up a readership at the LSE for The Australian National University Chair, given that in Canberra he would find it so much harder to stay in touch with leading scholars and practitioners in the arms control debate. In reply he pointed to the working advantages he would enjoy at The Australian National University by comparison with those of the LSE: more opportunities to travel, more study leave and fewer teaching obligations. He added that he probably would not stay in Canberra for the rest of his working life.

And so it happened. Bruce Miller in 1969 invited me to forsake the teaching of military history at the Royal Military College, Duntroon, and join his department as a senior fellow. I arrived two years after Hedley and quickly learned to work with him on a number of fronts. He was keen that I should take over the headship of the newly founded Strategic and Defence Studies Centre (SDSC) from its then head, Tom Millar. Tom had just taken on the Directorship of the Australian Institute of International Affairs, holding the two positions simultaneously. Tom had not foreseen such pressures to bring a newcomer into his position in the Centre, but Hedley and Bruce had a clear plan in mind and it was implemented with effect from the beginning of 1971.

While the work of the SDSC was focused largely on Asian and Pacific security issues (the Vietnam War was still in progress), I was keen to give it more of a global and a theoretical perspective. This took time, not least because Hedley was away on study leave in 1971–72 and I had my first study leave in 1973. The following year seemed a good time for holding a major conference on global security issues and I sought Hedley's advice on a topic for the gathering. He had already been thinking of the need for new ideas to be developed for discussion at the first review conference to be held under terms of the Nuclear Non-Proliferation Treaty in 1975. He put that set of issues forward as a policy-related matter to which we as academics could make a contribution, while at the same time we might be able to develop a dialogue with several of the key arms control specialists from the Australian Departments of Defence and Foreign Affairs. I was happy to take up his suggestion and develop a conference accordingly.

The Centre had been augmented by the arrival of Des Ball who knew more than most about the American strategic missile program, its purposes and the political debate around the topic in the United States. Jim Richardson and Geoff Jukes had already followed Hedley to The Australian National University from the Foreign Office. Harry Gelber at Monash University was an expert in Chinese nuclear matters, Peter King at the University of Sydney was working on the Strategic Arms Limitation negotiations and Arthur Burns (also at The Australian National University) had focused his work on great power relations, including their strategic nuclear policies. I invited them all to present papers and we thus had a credible team for an ambitious project. With those academics and a good mixture of government officials, foreign diplomats based in Canberra, relevant journalists and other academics, we held the conference on 24 and 25 July 1974. I edited the proceedings as the Centre's first book (*The Strategic Nuclear Balance; an Australian Perspective*) and it appeared early in 1975.

For the purpose of this chapter I shall focus on Hedley's contribution to that volume because it was succinct and wide-ranging, covering all of the major nuclear weapons issues before national governments in the 1970s and 1980s. He, of course, in the years since the publication of *The Control of the Arms Race*, had continued to write articles and papers for bodies such as the IISS (no longer just the ISS) and leading international journals on the broader issues not only of arms control but also of world order. He brought his thinking as of mid-1974 together in a concluding address to the conference.[3]

Bull (in this address) regarded the trend of world events as troubling in that an increased emphasis was being placed on nuclear weapons both by those states which had them (through technological advances, increased accuracy, reduction in sizes of warheads and so forth) and by those who aspired to have them, among which he included India. 'The nuclearisation of international politics appears to have accelerated.' His outlook generally was pessimistic: there was little prospect of nuclear disarmament, but the stability of deterrent balances should not be taken for granted. We were headed for trouble, he argued, and salvation lay only in three sets of measures which the international community, especially the nuclear weapons states, might take.

First, the nuclear weapons states had to put these systems more into the background of their strategic policies. To Bull this seemed unlikely and events of the 1980s (the deployment of intermediate–range nuclear weapons in Europe, the unveiling of President Reagan's plan for strategic defences, and the general high profile of debate on the relative strengths and war fighting capacities of American and Russian nuclear weapons) proved him to be correct.

Second, potential proliferators had to exert greater restraint. The obstacles in their path (lack of technical knowledge, cost and strength of the nuclear guarantees offered by friendly nuclear weapon states) were diminishing and the example that had been set by India through its 'peaceful nuclear explosion (PNE)', which occurred only two months before the conference, was a further stimulus to proliferation. Bull thought the stated rationale for the PNE, economic gain, was contemptible whereas security was a perfectly respectable objective for India (and others—like the existing nuclear weapons states) to attempt to achieve. As we have seen over the past two decades, a number of potential proliferators (including South Africa and Libya) have, after taking serious thought, abandoned their nuclear weapons projects. Restraint remains a potent factor. But several other states (including Iraq, India, Pakistan, Iran and North Korea) have gone in the opposite direction, opting for strengthened military security over restraint. We in the early twenty-first century now stand before the prospect of possession of nuclear weapons becoming the norm for middle powers in troubled regions. Tensions between restraint and the desire to have nuclear weapons remain strong and break-out by more potential proliferators is a definite possibility. Thus Bull's second requirement for a better foundation for international security has not been fulfilled.

Third, he argued, the Nuclear Non-Proliferation Treaty (an 'already tottering structure') needed to be strengthened. Bull recognised that further proliferation would take place: 'it is not credible that the most destructive weapons of the age will remain permanently the monopoly of the handful of states that first developed them.' The most feasible aim for the NPT regime was to slow the process of proliferation down, and this required not only the co-operation of the nuclear weapons states through keeping these weapons off centre stage, but also awareness on the part of potential proliferators that the more states had them, the more difficult it would be to inhibit their use in war. On the other hand, Bull recognised, it was pointless to preach nuclear abstinence to India or other proliferators who had already decided that they heeded nuclear weapons to strengthen their security and independence. 'If nuclear weapons were not important in enabling states to provide for their security, their prestige or their national independence, the problem of controlling the spread of nuclear weapons would be more easily soluble than it is.'

Thus Bull left us with no optimistic prospect. The thrust of his arguments was that the nuclear weapons states were unlikely to disarm; proliferation was likely to continue, albeit slowly; the NPT regime would continue to totter; and the world would move slowly to a more dangerous condition with more and more hands on a nuclear button. He characterised his own view as being based 'on general grounds of historical pessimism' and he was right in choosing this basis of argument. The long-term prospect for reduction of the nuclear threat 34 years later remains bleak, probably even bleaker than it was in 1974. Bull, at least, did not have to analyse international security developments in an era like that of the present, in which it is possible that terrorists might gain possession of nuclear warheads. These extremely destructive weapons in the hands of people who are perfectly willing to die in their attempts to injure their enemies, and for whom deterrence has no meaning because they lack any essential base whose security has to be preserved, have created a new and very serious dimension to the nuclear threat. Bull's 'historical pessimism' remains a fitting *leitmotiv* for the future as far as nuclear weapons are concerned.

Bull's work was certainly not a political platform for those activists such as those of the Campaign for Nuclear Disarmament who wanted to boost their following by attacking the causes of public neuroses. Rather, he provided a deeply informed and realist brief for those who had to bear the burden of international negotiations. Time and again he was to point out the futility of railing at nuclear weapons states and those who were on their way to achieving this status. In a matter as crucial as national security, government leaders were most unlikely to be swayed by foreign opinion, particularly that which emanated from liberal-thinking non-governmental organisations which had nothing with which to trade in the field of nuclear weapons policy. On the other hand he left us with this cheerless prospect of further proliferation, a weakening NPT regime and obduracy on the parts of existing nuclear weapons states. It is not surprising that humankind has not lain down and accepted this philosophy. Change might be very hard to achieve by way of nuclear disarmament, but something has to be attempted, many have argued and many more will continue to argue into the future.

As Montague Burton Professor at Oxford

By 1976 Bull had published most of his work on arms control. His focus had shifted to the nature of international order. His second book, *The Anarchical Society: A Study of Order in World Politics*,[4] appeared in 1977 at the time of his re-location to Oxford, succeeding Alastair Buchan as the Montague Burton Professor of International Relations. He was to move increasingly into the realms of the international society of states and away from those of international security. However he did remain active in the International Institute for Strategic Studies and was a powerful source of advice and ideas on the Institute's own endeavours in the late 1970s and 1980s to analyse the arms control problems of the SALT and START eras. Both I and my predecessor as Director of the Institute, Christoph Bertram, found his counsel invaluable because Hedley always had new ideas to impart

His work on arms control as a whole was based on his belief that the great powers would continue to compete for control in international affairs, and that the developing states would refuse to accept the injustices inflicted on them as newcomers to the international system. He also had a keen awareness for what Government leaders and their advisers would tolerate and accept from others by way of serious argument and criticism applied to their own policies. He abjured the more technical aspects of the arms control debate which came to the fore as weapons and missile technology continued to develop. He was no believer in strategic defences, arguing that if effective they would make nuclear war more rational and hence more probable.

Bull's work in this field demonstrates how far a very intelligent and logical person could progress in a new field of international security. As arms control was really developed only in the 1950s and 1960s, it was a topic on which a newcomer could make rapid progress, but few managed to approach Bull's standard of work. Many were drawn into the field because they had clear policy aims: usually to eliminate nuclear weapons or, less frequently, to utilise nuclear superiority to limit and weaken the other side. Bull initially lacked the usual background of experience in government or the armed forces. His area of academic knowledge was more philosophical and historical than political. The opportunity he had to work with Alastair Buchan, Michael Howard, and other senior persons in the ISS team was a major advantage, but he would not have gone far had his colleagues not been highly impressed by his qualities of thought and argument. This background, plus the publication of *The Control of the Arms Race* while he was still young (30 years of age), put him in an excellent position to establish arms control as a policy specialty within the British Foreign Office. The contacts he then made across NATO Europe and on the other side of the Atlantic, together with the ideas he drew from them for comparison with his own, equipped him to remain a leading arms control thinker on the world stage for the following decade and on some matters even longer.

Even moving to Australia in the late 1970s did not cut him off from active participation in the North Atlantic debate, because he continued to have excellent travel opportunities and a year of study leave in both 1971 and 1975. There was no Internet in those days of course, but airmail and the telephone played important roles for Hedley as he settled into his new working environment in the late 1960s.

By the mid-1970s Bull found that arms control had lost some of its fascination. He travelled increasingly to India and became both interested in and impressed by the arguments of leading Indian scholars on the need for reform in the international system, such as it was then. Coming from a former British imperial dominion himself, Bull had some natural sympathy for the underdogs in international politics and began to ask himself by what right did mainly Western, white European great powers, or those derived from them such as the United States, dominate in international councils and derive greater benefits from the existing world order than the poorer, newly independent states of Asia, Africa and Latin America. His work on the nature of international society led him into the two major projects at Oxford which each resulted in edited books: *The Expansion of International Society* and *Intervention in World Politics*.

During the late 1970s and early 1980s Bull also came to believe that the US alliance system was in decline. And indeed it was subject to a great deal of internal friction during these years, as the Reagan Administration began to re-emphasise US military power and his Administration's willingness to use force. Bull sided with those European leaders who claimed a stronger role in shaping alliance policy, and emphasised the second track of the 'twin-track' approach to relations with the Warsaw Pact which NATO claimed to have adopted: increased willingness to negotiate, especially to control the numbers and types of weapons envisaged for both deterrence and operational use. Bull argued that a bigger effort to achieve more comprehensive arms control agreements would be essential to the gaining and retention of public support for NATO policies in Western Europe. Fortunately the Americans took some note of the strength of these attitudes among their European allies, and in the mid and late 1980s adopted a less strident line. Sadly most of this re-orientation of policy took place after Bull's death in 1985.

In 1983, Bull returned to arms control, giving a final overview of the five ideas (which he believed to have been the essence of the new approach of 1958–61) in his well-known article 'The Classical Approach to Arms Control Twenty Years After'. The five ideas were:

- Arms control is not an end in itself but a means to an end—namely security against nuclear war.
- Arms control depends for its success on there being some perceived area of common interest between the antagonistic powers.
- Arms control and defence strategy are not mutually contradictory by nature and must be developed in harmony within the framework of an overall security policy.
- Arms control embraces a wider area of military policy than simply that which is covered by formal agreements.
- The most important immediate goal of arms control is to stabilise the relationship of mutual deterrence between the superpowers.

These five ideas remain of high relevance, notwithstanding the collapse of the Soviet Union and the Warsaw Pact. The West might no longer stand in danger of suffering defeat at the hands of a massive Warsaw Pact conventional force, but recent events in the Middle East point to the limitations on Western and particularly US conventional fighting power. While many may think that nuclear weapons no longer have any justifiable role in international politics and that we would be better off without them, we are a long way from this view being adopted by Western governments. In the meantime, as the framework of international order comes under attack by sub-national extremist groups, the menace of nuclear weapons to the leading powers of the current system grows increasingly strong.

As mentioned above, Bull remained active in the International Institute for Strategic Studies, serving both as a Council member and a member of the Executive Committee. As his illness became more serious in 1984–85, if anything he increased his level of participation in the Institute's work. I do not think he missed a meeting of either Council or Executive Committee in his last several months of life, even though he was weary and sometimes in pain. He gave everyone he came into contact with in those days heart to tackle more effectively whatever problems were absorbing their attention and energy. He remains an example in so many ways for all who were fortunate to work with him over three decades and more.

Bull's impact in the field of arms control policy was, on the whole, an indirect one. His work for the British Foreign Office is an exception to this judgement, of course, but he was in the British Government's service for just over two years. He will be remembered for his contributions to conferences of leading specialists, his journal articles, *The Control of the Arms Race*, his informal conversations with many who were in government service and above all for his teaching. At Oxford he had an opportunity to teach outstanding graduate students from around the world about international security and arms control. There are many who are still in the service of foreign and defence ministries, armed services, news media, universities and research institutes or, like myself, now in the ranks of the retired, who will always be grateful to Hedley Bull for the quality of his thought, his critical abilities and willingness to use them, his ready sense of humour and his intellectual energy. He was a rare phenomenon and deserves to be remembered and held in the highest regard. On looking at his independence and impact, it is not difficult to see why he made his colleagues feel proud to have chosen the same profession and field as himself.[5]

ENDNOTES

[1] For the text of Hedley Bull's review of *The Arms Race* see his 'Disarmament and the International System' *The Australian Journal of Politics and History*, vol. 5, no. 1, May 1959 or Chapter Two of *Hedley Bull on Arms Control*, Macmillan, London, 1987, selected and introduced by Robert O'Neill and David Schwartz. This second volume is an anthology of Bull's main writings on arms control. It does not pretend to be a complete coverage of Bull's work in this field.

[2] Michael Howard, *Captain Professor: A Life in War and Peace*, Continuum, London, 2006 p. 165.

[3] Robert O'Neill (ed.), *The Strategic Nuclear Balance: An Australian Perspective*, Strategic and Defence Studies Centre, The Australian National University, 1975, pp. 130–48. Hedley Bull re-wrote this address and published it in *International Affairs*, vol 51, April 1975, pp. 175–84, under the title 'Rethinking Non-Proliferation'.

[4] Hedley Bull, *The Anarchical Society: A Study of Order in World Politics*, Macmillan, London and Basingstoke, 1977.

[5] The author is grateful to Mrs Mary Bull for her comments on the first draft of this chapter and for the additional information she provided.

Chapter 4

London: the LSE, the 'British Committee on International Theory', the 'English School' and the early days of the IISS

Coral Bell

London in the ten years from 1965 to 1975 seemed to me the central focus of intellectual enquiry about issues of war and peace. Washington was under rather a cloud because of its increasing, and disastrous, involvement in Vietnam. Hedley and I both taught at the London School of Economics (LSE), though not during the same period. We were both members of the British Committee on International Theory, the so-called 'English School', and also of what became the now worldwide International Institute for Strategic Studies (IISS). In its earliest days it was mostly a London-based association, operating out of just a couple of rooms in the Adelphi. Hedley acquired a second base in the Foreign Office, when Harold Wilson came into office as Prime Minister, and I had one at Chatham House, the Royal Institute of International Affairs. Those years in London were enormously important to me, and I think to Hedley as well, so they seem to deserve the recording of a few memories.

The most vital thing about the LSE, aside from the students, for both Hedley and me, was the influence of Martin Wight, but I have included in this book Hedley's own memorial lecture to him, so I think I do not need to say much more here about his great charisma as both teacher and colleague. But it seems worthwhile to say a few words about the changes in both the LSE itself and the general context in which strategic issues and crisis-management were discussed in London in the six years or so between my arrival as a graduate student in 1951 and Hedley's as an assistant lecturer. In retrospect, those years seem to mark an important shift in the context of discussion of all the Cold War issues, some of which are still with us, and certainly were with Hedley to the end of his life.

When I arrived in 1951, London was a city barely getting over a war. Its ruins lay all about us. I stayed for a while in a student place in Bloomsbury and used to walk on Sundays down to St Pauls, still rising triumphantly above a small wilderness of a pretty pink-blossomed wildflower called *London Pride*. It all seemed tremendously symbolic.

So did some events in the academic and political fields. One was that the Attlee Government, which had inherited power from Churchill just before the end of the war, was by then reaching the end of its own days. So was the brave but forlorn Festival of Britain. And so was the reign of Harold Laski, who had been regarded by many as the conscience of the British Labour Party, as well as the dominant intellectual force at the LSE and in the British Left in general, for many years. By this time he had come to be quite a thorn in the side of the Prime Minister, who, once (in a letter adroitly 'leaked') had famously advised him, 'a period of silence from you would be appreciated'.

At the LSE he was succeeded by Michael Oakeshott, as famous and influential a figure on the traditionalist Right as Laski had been on the Left. *The New Statesman* regarded it as a great betrayal, and raged about the appointment for weeks. I was luckily in time to catch the last of Laski's lectures and the Oakeshott inaugural. Some of that inaugural lecture has helped define international politics for me ever since.

All that may sound like mere academic small change now, more than half a century afterwards. But, in retrospect, it still really does mark a change in the intellectual climate of Europe, and maybe the West generally. Of course the Cold War had been with us since March 1946, and already had its classics in the literature of international relations. (My first seminar paper for Martin Wight was on Kennan's theory of containment.) But a further turn in disillusionment, from some at least of the more optimistic assumptions of the wartime Left, meant more permanent acceptance that the optimism of the past had to be discarded, in fields like the control of the arms race, a point quite important in Hedley's early success, and in the development of the IISS, which was so vital an influence to him.

Of course, it did not translate at the time to the intellectual atmosphere of the Research Common Room, which was where I found my company for the next few years. I still remember the President of that cosmopolitan body, a charming Iraqi, welcoming newcomers (of whom I was one) as recruits to an institution 'which had given so many brave young men to the revolutionary forces of the world'. True enough. Not many of my friends have been executed by firing squad, or been the target of political assassination. But the little group of six or seven I used to hang out with in those years included one of each: an Iranian who grew up to be Mayor of Teheran, and was executed by the Ayatollah's regime, and an Israeli who got to be Ambassador in London, and luckily survived his intended murder for political reasons.

Philosophically, the LSE at the beginning of my time as a student there was dominated by Professor Karl Popper, whose book *The Open Society and Its Enemies* is still as powerfully relevant to the struggle against authoritarianism in these days of fundamentalist religious doctrine, as in those days of fundamentalist political doctrines. But in time I came to be more influenced by the delicate ironic scepticism and pragmatism of Oakeshott:

In political activity, then, men sail a bottomless and boundless sea; there is neither harbour for shelter nor floor for anchorage, neither starting-place nor appointed destination. The enterprise is to keep afloat on an even keel; the sea is both friend and enemy, and seamanship consists in using the resources of a traditional manner of behaviour to make a friend of every inimical occasion.[1]

Those words, from his inaugural lecture, have always seemed to me to define particularly the dilemmas of international politics. But I am not sure whether Hedley was equally influenced.

As far as the British Committee on International Theory is concerned, the primary thing to bear in mind is that its name was rather a misnomer. It was really not a committee, but an old-fashioned small discussion group, in an Oxford and Cambridge tradition. It did not aim to build or present a body of international theory. Indeed, Martin Wight, one of the two 'stars' of the groups (Hedley was the other) once published a provocative little essay called 'Why is there no international theory', evoking blasts of indignation from many of his academic colleagues, especially as he rather implied that there was not likely to be one either.

I was a member of the group from the time I was recruited in 1965 as Reader in International Affairs at the LSE until 1977, when I returned to The Australian National University. For those 12 years, the group was a major intellectual influence on my life, especially because of the times it provided for talking to Hedley and Martin. Its ending has been a long grief, even though we only met two or three weekends a year. On average, I think there were usually only about eight people present on most of those occasions. We met in a Cambridge or Oxford College during student vacations.

The group had been founded in 1958, convened initially by Herbert Butterfield, a historian perhaps less well-known now than he was then—the originator of what was then called 'the Whig interpretation of history'. Originally it was financed, along with a similar group in the United States, by the Rockefeller Foundation, which covered the then very modest costs of our food and lodging. Once, I remember, we met at a grand Italian palace, at Bellagio on Lake Como, which is maintained by the Foundation to provide an occasional taste of luxury to needy scholars.

One of the ideas behind the group was that the meetings would provide a chance for the academic analysts of policy to meet those who actually made it—foreign office people and such. I think that worked reasonably well, but the only members of whom I retain vivid memories were Hedley, Martin, Michael Howard and Adam Watson. Adam had been the British Ambassador in Cuba, and was to be Hedley's most important editorial collaborator later.

Though the Cold War was in full vigour for the entire lifetime of the group, we were much less concerned with that than with the intellectual history of political thought, insofar as it was directed towards issues of war and peace. So we were more preoccupied with Thucydides, or Sun Tzu, or Hobbes, or Machiavelli, or Kant or Burke, or Tom Paine or Lenin than with the latest developments between Moscow and Washington. Or, rather, what we were trying for was an understanding of how the books of those who had written most perceptively about similar dilemmas in their respective times could help us comprehend and illuminate ours. I remember the last thing Martin said to me, just before his sudden and lamentably early death, was that he was returning to Grotius, and finding him more relevant to contemporary events (this was 1972) than he had expected.

In Martin's last year or two, we had been brooding a good deal over the transformation of the original European society of states into a global and universal society of states, but it was not until Hedley had taken over as a sort of discussion leader that we decided on the study that became eventually *The Expansion of International Society*, as a venture that many of us, as well as relevant outside scholars, would write essays for. Hedley and Adam became joint editors, and it occupied a good deal of their time over the next decade or so. Our timetables were leisurely in those distant days.

It was always intended that the book would be, not just a collection of individual essays, but a coherent and comprehensive account of that whole 500-year patch of history, from the end of the fifteenth century to the end of the twentieth century. So it was seen as a systematic analysis of that evolution, under four headings: the nature and expansion of the European system, the reaction against the world order thus created, the entry nevertheless of the non-European states into it, and the nature of the new global society—'the flood-tide of European dominance over the world, and its subsequent ebbing', as Hedley put it.

I think that we adhered to that notion reasonably well, and that gave a convincing and understandable shape to what might otherwise have been a rather undisciplined analysis. (I wrote the essay on China and the international order). Hedley and Adam wrote the introduction and conclusion together, and Hedley, despite gathering ill-health, wrote three of the essays—those on the revolt against the West, the emergence of a universal global society, and the Western collision with Africa.

To my mind, Hedley's work on this book is particularly important to Australians, including Canberra policymakers. His writings on the anarchical society, and control of the arms race, though immensely valuable, are likely to be read mostly by academic or expert groups. But *The Expansion of International Society* could be read without difficulty by high-school students, and should give them an understanding of 500 years of history—the world-historical process that provided the global context within which Australia emerged to its present status. The world is now changing very fast. In order to understand where that world is now going, it is helpful to understand where it came from.

The British Committee on International Theory in time mutated into what has now been called 'the English School' of international theory. That name also is a misnomer: owed to an unfriendly critic, from Aberystwyth, who suggested that it was high time we shut up shop. I used to wistfully think at times that it might be better, since other people seemed determined to give us a name, for us to start calling ourselves 'the London School of International and Strategic Theory'. 'London' does not carry any sense of being exclusively English or British: it is an immensely cosmopolitan city, even more so now than when we all met regularly there. A Londoner can be from Albania or Zimbabwe, and these days probably is. It always seemed to me that it was particularly incongruous that Hedley, who was so defiantly Australian, should come to be described as a member of the English school. However, Martin (who was certainly the primary focus of the English School, if one exists) did not take to strategic analysis. He had been a pacifist in his youth and, though he abandoned that position in time, he retained a revulsion against strategic analysis, especially nuclear calculations.

I had the good fortune to know three of the founding members of the IISS when the whole project was still just a gleam in the eyes of those who later became among its most eminent influences: Michael Howard, Denis Healey and Alastair Buchan. I was working in the early 1950s (though still a graduate student at the LSE) at Chatham House, originally as rapporteur on a book about Britain and the United Nations, and those three were members of the study-group for the book. All of them had fought hard wars. Alastair had been at the Arnhem disaster, and once told me that he had seen most of his friends die all around him. Denis had been beach-master at Anzio, one of the hardest-fought landings in Europe. Michael had fought his way through Europe with his regiment. All three had come to understand that war was too serious a matter to be left to the generals. This was the time when the full implications of the consequences of nuclear war were just beginning to be understood, even by the strategists.

Denis (now Lord Healey) in due course became the most influential spokesman in Parliament about strategic issues, especially nuclear ones, and Defence Minister in Harold Wilson's Government, when Labour came back into office in the 1960s. That was Hedley's time at the Foreign Office, working on arms control policy. Bob O'Neill's splendid essay in this volume is the best authority on that. In time, no doubt the Foreign Office archives will provide more documents. But I was for a while a member of an Advisory Committee of academics and others that Hedley set up, and I remember with great enjoyment its meetings. His Minister (a former Army officer who had become defence correspondent of *The Times*, and then Lord Chalfont when the Prime Minister needed a spokesman in the Lords) seemed to provide Hedley with quite a free hand. We listened to and argued with people like Patrick Blackett, the eminent physicist, whom many misguided people regarded as practically a traitor, because his views were so far left, on why Western policy was all wrong, and Lord Rothschild, the eminent zoologist, on the aggressive instinct in animals, including man. I do not know whether our deliberations helped Hedley, but they certainly improved my understanding of the political process, in London and elsewhere.

Hedley, to all our grief, died in 1985, just after the publication of the hard-cover edition of *The Expansion of International Society* and I think the rest of us were so depressed by the early loss of our two stars, both at the peak of their intellectual vitality, that it seemed the right moment to let the group itself fade into memory. But it still has some resonance in the field. I once heard a young Chinese scholar, at a seminar in Canberra, present Beijing's grappling with the line of thought we had been working on. For me, those long-ago meetings will always be among the happiest and most valuable experiences of my life. As will the earliest meetings of the IISS.

Alastair Buchan, who ran the Institute single-handedly (save for one faithful secretary) in those days, knew just about everyone in the relevant 'Establishment' (I once saw the then Archbishop of Canterbury at any early meeting). Policymakers came to talk to us, only 20 or so people, round a single table bearing some sandwiches and wine. The Mandarins would drift up from Whitehall, and the rest of us down from the LSE or Fleet Street, or Australia House or King's College. Alastair himself died grievously early, as had Martin and as Hedley himself and a younger colleague John Vincent, were to do. I know that Hedley valued and mourned him as much as I did. Sometimes I felt that the gods were fighting against us, through those grievous losses from our common endeavour to secure rational policies in the Cold War. But disaster was avoided in that conflict, and may with luck be avoided again in the new world dilemmas that now confront policymakers. The stream of intellectual analysis that goes back to Thucydides and Sun Tzu flows on still.

ENDNOTES

[1] Michael Joseph Oakeshott, 'Political Education'. Inaugural lecture at the London School of Economics, delivered on 6 March 1951.

Chapter 5

'A Common Interest in Common Interest': Hedley Bull, Thomas Schelling and Collaboration in International Politics

Robert Ayson

Hedley Bull wrote his modern classic *The Anarchical Society* in the office long occupied by the incumbent Professor of International Relations at The Australian National University. The holder of that post is now situated in the Hedley Bull Centre alongside us strategic studies people, for whom Bull stands as an important thinker in our own peculiar subject.[1] In particular, Bull's 1968 essay in *World Politics*, 'Strategic Studies and its Critics'[2] remains unsurpassed in its elegance and power, and in its attempt to defend the academic subject which some regarded then, and may still regard today, as morally and intellectually indefensible.

Thomas Schelling is one of the most influential, and certainly one of the most original, strategic thinkers of the nuclear age. Two years ago he was awarded a Nobel Prize in economics, the subject in which he was educated. But the prize was really for his contributions in applied political economy, celebrating his contributions to the understanding of the processes of international conflict. The main work in which he established this reputation, *The Strategy of Conflict*, was published in 1960, a decade and a half before Bull's *Anarchical Society* appeared. *The Strategy of Conflict* is essential and provocative reading for anyone wanting to think seriously about strategy as a process of interdependent decision. It remains often cited in the international relations literature as well as in other fields.

This chapter is a preliminary exploration of a common interest in common interest which is apparent in the work of these two scholars. My analysis falls into two main parts. First, I will examine the roughly comparable locations of these two scholars in middle ground between pure cooperation and pure conflict in great power relations. Second, I will demonstrate the interest the two scholars had in each other's work in the mid-1960s as a possible, although partial, explanation for this intellectual convergence. I will conclude by commenting briefly on signs that Bull and Schelling were both attracted by the possibility of going beyond a mix of cooperation and competition in international politics to situations where pure coordination and cosmopolitan norms might just prevail.

Theorists of the Productive Middle Ground

Hedley Bull and Thomas Schelling can both be regarded as theorists of the middle ground. I do not mean to say that their work is neither one thing nor the other. I am not implying that their scholarship would appeal to Goldilocks who preferred baby bear's porridge because it was neither too hot nor too cold but 'just right'. Because of their sheer intellectual energy Bull and Schelling probably escape the academic version of the judgment heaped on the Church of Laodicea through John's revelation from God that 'because you are lukewarm—neither hot nor cold—I am about to spit you out of my mouth'.[3]

Instead Bull and Schelling manage to mark out a powerful theoretical middle ground between rival and rather extreme positions on the nature of international politics. The similar location they occupy explains the richness of their respective contributions. However this similarity may not be immediately obvious given the differences in the language they use and also in their disciplinary backgrounds.

Bull's international society approach falls in between the unrelenting conflict of Hobbesian realism and the utopian harmony of Kantian universalism. As Bull explains it in his best known work: 'International politics, in the Grotian understanding, expresses neither complete conflict of interest between states nor complete identity of interest: it resembles a game that is partly distributive but also partly productive.'[4] His comments at a 1962 meeting of the British Committee on the Theory of International Politics offer an especially useful explanation of this approach and are worth quoting at some length:

> Grotius, you will recall, wrote in the situation of international anarchy in which the authority of divine law had broken down; in which the positive law, as it were, of Pope and Emperor had broken down; and in which there were really two views in the field; on the one hand the Machiavellian view that because there was no superior authority over sovereign states, there was really therefore no law or no authority binding on sovereign princes; and the other view ... that the only way to get order among princes was to re-establish some kind of universal state—to re-establish some sort of superior authority. ... Now Grotius was trying to produce a third alternative between these two conceptions, and he found it in the notion that there was an international society—a society of states—which was morally binding and which was a real force even in the absence of any superior authority. The main grounds for his asserting the validity of such a system was his attempt to restate the

doctrine of Natural Law: that there were moral and legal rules which were natural in the sense that they did not derive from God, and in the sense that they were not positive and did not derive from human will, but were obvious to all human beings.[5]

Bull's formulation of the mix of conflict and cooperation in international politics, which I quoted before this longer extract, could easily have been written by Schelling, although he might have said it about strategic relationships specifically rather than international politics in general. Schelling did not identify himself with a particular International Relations tradition. He talked about his work in developing a theory of strategy in pioneering terms as 'something … that looks like a mixture of game theory, organization theory, communication theory, theory of evidence, theory of choice, and theory of collective decision'.[6] I remember my first interview with Schelling when he said that he had not been aware of the literature on the balance of power when he developed his thinking on stability, an accusation which could never be made of Bull. This made me revise my account of where Schelling's approach to stability came from (and to contrast it with the different origins of Bull's and Henry Kissinger's).[7]

Instead, Schelling's middle ground approach is best appreciated in terms of microeconomics, the subject in which he was educated. His theoretical focus is on bargaining processes in situations of oligopoly where there are only a few sellers in the market (more like the relationship between Qantas and Virgin Blue than between the many restaurants in Sydney). This results in situations of imperfect competition where behaviour lies somewhere in between the conditions of pure competition (where business survival can be a cut-throat affair) and pure control (where complete monopoly reigns).[8] These are Schelling's economic analogies of Bull's Hobbesian and Kantian worlds respectively.

Schelling uses this approach to understand strategy as a non-zero sum game (partly distributive and also partly productive) where actors are related to one another by a mixture of competition and cooperation in their interests and behaviour. These games are prevalent in relationships among actors who have the capacity to cause considerable harm to one another, and who in doing so would also damage themselves. In other words, these actors have a common interest in restraining the harm they cause one another, just as unionists and employers have a common interest in finding a bargain between their competing demands.

Bull and Schelling therefore have a common interest in common interest, albeit for somewhat uncommon academic reasons. For both authors, these common interests could be played out through informal institutions (that is, through patterns of collaborative behaviour) as well as (or in Schelling's case instead of) formal ones such as the United Nations. Schelling had a particular interest in tacit bargaining—where the parties would signal their intentions and agreement through their strategic behaviour rather than through any explicit formal agreement. Bull argued in a broader sense that order was quite possible without formal government. This assessment built on his reading of the anthropology of pre-modern African societies. At one stage he comments that 'international society is an anarchical society, a society without government. But primitive stateless societies also present this spectacle of "ordered anarchy".'[9] Contemporary social scientific research thus held an interest for Bull as well as for Schelling who was a wide and eclectic reader.

Both thinkers had a strong interest in consistent patterns of behaviour which could comprise these sometimes informal institutions. This is the basis for what Bull refers to as order, his central preoccupation as a theorist,[10] and for what Schelling refers to as stability. Schelling's fascination with stability—consistent patterns of behaviour around which the expectations and behaviour of strategic actors (such as states) could converge—relied heavily on the insight that these actors were bound together by interdependent relationships. As they interacted and began to appreciate the reciprocal nature of their relationship, patterns could form as the participants tacitly agreed on limits beyond which their behaviour should not be allowed to go.

For Bull, the interest in patterns of behaviour was also very strong. Kai Alderson and Andrew Hurrell write of the

> central idea in Bull's work that rules, laws and conventions can, and often do, emerge without an overarching authority on the basis of shared interests. They are of mutual benefit because they help shape expectations, increase the predictability of international life, and thereby reduce uncertainty and insecurity.[11]

We could substitute Schelling's name for Bull's here without doing any violence to either thinker.

But in Bull's work one gets the sense that the common interests between actors do not so much as follow from their interdependence and interaction but are a prior basis for it. Strongly influenced as he was by Martin Wight's emphasis on the importance of history in international affairs,[12] Bull argued that a strong historical basis, 'a common culture or civilisation', is required to 'underlie an international society'. The features involved here may include 'a common language, a common epistemology and understanding of the universe, a common religion, a common ethical code' which 'may make for easier communication and closer awareness and understanding between one state and another, and thus facilitate the definition of common rules and the evolution of common institutions' or 'may reinforce the sense of common interests that impels states to accept common rules and institutions with a sense of common values'.[13] In other words, a rich tapestry of collective experience and outlook allows for effective cooperation. The states involved might be regarded as *natural* collaborators because of this common history. This is certainly the impression one gains from Bull's appreciation of European international society.

Bull tends to define order as something distinct from the rules which contribute to it. The mere existence of limits on behaviour may not be sufficient for order. There needs to be an understanding of the broader purposes which shape the use of these rules. These goals may owe something to natural law, in the way Bull cites Grotius above,[14] even though in his early work Bull seemed to prefer the pluralism and positivism of another international lawyer, Lassa Oppenheim,[15] whose approach might just have appealed to Schelling. As Alderson and Hurrell write:

> Bull differed from US theorists of cooperation ... on the importance that he attached to the close study of state practice and to the historical processes by which understandings of common interest evolved and changed through time. ... Rationalist models of cooperation may indeed explain how cooperation is possible once the parties have come to believe that they form part of a shared project. ... But rational prudence alone cannot explain the initiation of the game and why each player individually might choose to begin to cooperate.[16]

Schelling's explanation for the patterns of collaboration between states who observe common rules is more ahistorical and social scientific. At times he may stray close to being included in Bull's criticism 'that the practitioners of the scientific approach [to international relations], by cutting themselves off from history and philosophy, have ... a view of their subject and its possibilities that is callow and brash',[17] even though Bull numerously indicated he regarded Schelling as a scientific theorist who rose above some of these problems. For Schelling, the great power collaboration which mattered most, between the Cold War foes the United States and the Soviet Union, arose from a largely blank canvas. They had antithetical politics and what they lacked in communication they more than made up for in mutual suspicion. They were not natural collaborators by any stretch of the imagination. But they could still be expected to work together. Bull's European great powers were longstanding dance partners; Schelling's superpowers were going on a rather risky blind date.

Schelling faced a somewhat uphill battle in selling the argument that the two superpower adversaries could be expected to cooperate, writing as he was in the tenser portions of the Cold War in the late 1950s and early 1960s. Here he relied heavily on the logic of deductive reasoning (as opposed to inductive studies drawn from observing detailed superpower behaviour which would have appealed more to Bull). For example, one of his sources for the argument that potentially competitive actors could stabilise their behaviour around focal points came in the form of the completely unrelated experiments conducted in the 1930s by the social psychologist Muzafer Sherif who had asked participants to identify the location of a point of light shining onto a screen.[18] These findings indicated that the differences between individual estimations of the point's location were reduced significantly when the same individuals were operating as a group. In others words, when interaction occurred, convergence around common norms became likely. This allows what scholars have come to call strategic learning[19]—a phenomenon Bull also believed was possible,[20] although not necessarily for the same reasons.

For Schelling, the act of interaction (even between states with little naturally or historically in common) could produce its own culture and common values which underlies cooperation and thus stability. This seems the opposite of Bull where the common values precede the cooperation. In Schelling's theorising, where stability depends on the extent to which common rules are observed, the act of restraint, the limit itself, is essentially equivalent to order. If one finds a pattern of behaviour, if one finds behaviour conducted within limits, one has found stability.[21] One can even find order in conflict itself. Actors who are fighting one another do not necessarily miss out on order because of the obvious evidence of a record of violence between them: they can still find order within the conflict process. Indeed, Schelling noted in an interview that the steady state of violence on the western front in the First World War constituted stability.

For Bull, war is one of the institutions of international society[22] which contributes to order as a 'means of enforcing international law, of preserving the balance of power, and, arguably, of promoting changes in the law generally regarded as just.'[23] Once again there is a separation between the ingredients for order and the order itself. Bull is explicit here about the political uses of, and constraints on, violence. This corresponds rather well to the relationship between military means and political ends, and the ideas of limited war, we can find in Clausewitz. For Schelling, stability existed within the microeconomics of violence rather than in the broader system of international politics—closer to the interactive side of Clausewitz's writings on strategy where war can have a logic all of its own. Schelling focused on the potential for violent (or other harmful) interaction to explode and on the need for restraint to ensure this did not happen. He identified that restraint with decisions on the way in which violence was threatened and applied, and not back to the broader purposes of international society. The political implications are in the background, but they tend to be assumed rather than spelled out.

While Schelling's analysis is also less historically informed than Bull's, it does allow for the significance of track records. For example, earlier resting places or bargains can act as precedents which guide the stabilisation of future behaviour. In the writing where he first explores his theory of bargaining, Schelling draws upon his experience working in the Marshall Plan authority in Europe to suggest that the allocation of foreign assistance had a tendency to following earlier patterns.[24] Whether these allocations were a good outcome for all concerned was not the point; even an arbitrary and undeserved distribution of benefits might act as a self-reinforcing precedent which can shape future behaviour, although notions of fairness (for example, a natural 50/50 split) can come into play but more because of their salience than their justice. For Bull, however, order is much more than following a mere pattern: At the start of *The Anarchical Society*, he argues:

> The order which men look for in social life is not any pattern or regularity in the relations of human individuals or groups, but a pattern that leads to a particular result, an arrangement of social life such that it promotes certain goals or values.[25]

And in the build-up to this passage he argues that 'a pattern may be evident in the behavior of men or groups of men in violent conflict with one another, yet this situation we should characterise as disorderly.'[26]

For Bull, order needed to be a good pattern. Indeed Bull argues that 'states in the Grotian view are bound not only by rules of prudence or expediency but also by imperatives of morality and law'.[27] Stanley Hoffman writes that 'Bull's concern for international society and his interest in moral conceptions are inextricably linked'.[28] One does find a similar demarcation in Schelling's work between patterns in general and those particular patterns which involved order; one could expect that the former meant the latter. Schelling once told me that stability was a popular word because of the assumption that it implies something beneficial, whereas it was really an objective characteristic of all sorts of systems. He was willing to attribute the quality of stability to almost any pattern in any situation, including into war itself. Hence Schelling's rather controversial interest in intrawar deterrence, which is not too far from Herman Kahn's colourful and almost unbelievable explorations of the dynamics of nuclear exchanges. Even so, this work might be defended on the basis that such deterrence might limit the further spread of violence beyond the initial nuclear exchange. Indeed it can be argued that Schelling had certain purposes for these patterns in mind: the deterrence of initial war and the limitation of any subsequent violence based on a clear pattern which reinforces those limits.

The appeal of almost any pattern in Schelling's universe does not mean that stability is a naturally occurring phenomenon which turns up almost by accident. It is not like the Newtonian and pre-Napoleonic view of a self-correcting balance of power where the great states mirrored the self-maintaining positions of the planets.[29] Schelling's working assumption was that strategic actors tended to behave rationally and certainly purposefully as they sought to enhance their interests. These actors could be expected rather to utilise, construct, and even manipulate patterns which supported those purposes, although there was always going to be a bargain between the varying self-interest of the participating actors. Schelling did not expect these actors always and everywhere to act rationally. But as an economist, even a heterodox one, he was still inclined to view such an assumption as a useful starting point: 'The premise of "rational behavior" is a potent one for the production of theory. Whether the resulting theory provides good or poor insight into actual behavior is … a matter for subsequent judgment.'[30] Some of Schelling's detractors who regarded him as a dangerous mathematician of violence[31] may have ignored this subtle but important distinction.

One can find an outwardly very similar logic in Bull's comment that the assumption of rationality, at work in much American international relations thinking was 'only good for formal theorising'.[32] But Bull's qualification is much more serious than Schelling's. This is not so much because Bull entirely dismissed the sort of formal theory which Schelling found useful. As James L. Richardson has pointed out, Bull was at times an admirer of aspects of the behaviourist turn in American international relations thinking which at other times he seemed all too happy to debunk.[33] But it is certainly the case that formal theory had far less appeal to Bull who (with the rest of the English School) did not tend to indulge in it. And there were times when he felt that the formal theorists were asking rather too much of real-life strategic actors.

Bull's most memorable and quoted passage on that subject is his comment that the rational strategic man is 'a man who on further acquaintance reveals himself as a university professor of unusual intellectual subtlety'.[34] It is more than a little likely that he had Schelling in mind when making this comment. In an essay written ten years later, Bull repeats this splendid line and then adds:

> I have also criticised Schelling's theories about force and bargaining, which are primarily and consciously an extrapolation of 'rational strategic action', on the ground that he is inclined to confuse them with descriptions of actual situations and with policy prescriptions.[35]

This criticism came in Bull's review of Schelling's *Arms and Influence*. This ambitious book takes the bargaining theory developed in *The Strategy of Conflict* and extends it almost to breaking point in suggesting the possibilities of exploiting the power to hurt. Schelling's brilliance in making these arguments was not in doubt. But Bull argues that

> there can be no substitute for studying the record of what the governments of the United States, the Soviet Union, the United Kingdom, China, and France actually do and think. Principles of strategic 'rationality' can help us frame hypotheses about this record but we must resist the temptation to use them as a shortcut.[36]

Such a comment might be made about all sorts of theoretical reasoning in international relations and strategic studies.

Bull's circumspection about rationality reflected his education in disciplines other than economics. As Stanley Hoffman argues:

> Hedley Bull was no believer in the ordinary rationality of states, nor in the usefulness of developing prescriptions for rational action, because he was even more pessimistic than the realists. To them, departures from the norm are exceptions; to Hedley Bull, stupidity, folly, miscalculations, and mischief were always possible.[37]

Schelling wasn't really a realist either. Not because he was more pessimistic like Bull, but possibly because he was more optimistic than many realists given his assertion of the possibility for strategic cooperation in a way which might position his work as a preliminary to the hopes of the neoliberal institutionalists of the 1970s.

Schelling also recognised the possibility for mischief and miscalculation, including the parallels he drew between the crisis of August 1914 and those of the nuclear age.[38] He was concerned that the reciprocally reinforcing expectations and fears of the participants might so easily lead to the outcome that none of them might ordinarily wish for. But he still retained more faith than Bull in the innate rationality of strategic actors, partly because what was irrational for the international system as a whole could sometimes be the product of individual rationalities.[39] Stupid outcomes did not mean that the actors who contributed them were similarly unwise—there might be temptations to defect from mutually beneficial bargains which few actors could possibly resist. Rousseau's colourful stag-hunting metaphor of what would come to be called 'the prisoner's dilemma' makes the same suggestion.

Bull set higher standards against which he expected the great powers in particular to act, at least in principle. The great powers were the great responsibles (or at least ought to be) who, because of their privileged position and the unequal influence they wielded, had particular obligations to international order.[40] Historically, at certain times in the European states system (for example, the Concert of Europe) they had delivered on this potential. These same powers, to the extent that they formed an international society, could draw on common standards, rules and behaviour. But in practice Bull expected to be more disappointed because of the very frailty (and vainglory) of those actors in a way that any reader of the power politics literature might agree.

Schelling's norms were much more created than made. They could be introduced on the spot. From the Cuban missile crisis Schelling detected a tacit agreement by the Americans and Soviets, constrained by the awful consequences of a failure to limit their interaction, to prevent things from spreading beyond the confines of the Caribbean.[41] Norms of behaviour such as these might seem more wobbly than Bull's conventions which were part of an ongoing international society. Schelling's norms of behaviour did not come from a *noblesse oblige* built up historically in a society of states. Instead, in a thermonuclear age where the superpowers could blow most things to smithereens, the Americans and the Russians had little choice but to restrain their behaviour and keep restraining it. In *Arms and Influence*, Schelling argues:

> Now we are in an era in which the power to hurt … is commensurate with the power to take and to hold, perhaps more than commensurate, perhaps decisive, and it is even more necessary to think of warfare as a process of violent bargaining.[42]

Stability could rest on some rather ghastly foundations: Schelling compared the bargain implicit in mutual nuclear deterrence to the much older practice of exchanging hostages who would thus act rather like human shields.[43] But, precisely because Schelling was less demanding about the goodness of patterns (and at the same time more optimistic about the actors' capacity for observing them), he found more room for hope that conventions might be observed. The *logic* of restraint is thus stronger in Schelling's work.

The Bull–Schelling Connection

This is where the work of these two scholars connects in quite a direct way—in the creation of a system of rules for the management of the challenges of an age of nuclear weapons. This is not evident in Bull's *Anarchical Society*—which does not cite the then Harvard University Professor, but which cites Coral Bell, and the sometimes overlooked but brilliant work of Morton Kaplan, and misspells Samuel Huntington's surname. However, Bull's earlier and magisterial *Control of the Arms Race* contains the politically incorrect argument that 'the maintenance of a stable Soviet–Western balance may require high levels and advanced kinds of arguments, and may even be served by the further prosecution of the arms race in certain fields'.[44] His footnote to that point is as follows: 'The most persuasive exponent of these arguments has been Professor Thomas C. Schelling of Harvard University, to whose work on the theory of arms control, and especially on the problems of surprise attack, I an especially indebted.'[45] It is important to note here that Bull not only cited relevant parts of Schelling's *Strategy of Conflict*, but also two of Schelling's journal articles from 1960 which indicate he was an avid reader of the American strategist.

Bull had visited the east coast of the United States in September 1957 and met Schelling.[46] At that time the American thinker's work on strategic bargaining and the limitation of armed conflict was gaining influence through the publication of essays which were to find their way into *The Strategy of Conflict*. It was also the period in which Bull was rejecting the much more absolutist logic of complete disarmament which he had encountered as a scholar assisting the former British politician Philip Noel-Baker.[47] Bull's assault in 1959 on Noel-Baker's book, which had been published the previous year under the title *The Arms Race*, carries little direct sign of an awareness of Schelling's work,[48] but this influence was to become more apparent in Bull's work within the next two years.

Bull's *Control of the Arms Race*, officially the product of an Institute for Strategic Studies working group, but really the work of the author, found an admirer in Schelling who reviewed it in pre-publication form for the Institute's new journal *Survival*. Schelling found it to be a 'cool and competent envelopment of recent strategic thinking in a political treatise on international violence'.[49] He applauded the 'genius' of Bull's book in putting 'the problem of war in political, historical, and moral perspective'[50]—something the reviewer himself could not have been accused of doing. But it is evident that Schelling considered himself the more original thinker. He argues that 'Bull's careful analysis turns up no new ideas', and might even have been thinking of his own *Strategy of Conflict* in arguing that, had Bull published a year earlier, it 'would have been unique in its application of military reasoning to arms control'.[51]

This is not an opinion shared by all. Robert O'Neill and David Schwartz, who two decades ago edited a retrospective volume containing Bull's main works on arms control, call him 'one of its most original and penetrating contributors'.[52] Even so, a contrast can be made from 1961 between Hedley Bull, a young scholar not yet 30 whose broader ideas on international relations were still evolving, and Thomas Schelling, ten years his senior, who had by that time erected an enduring and mature framework of strategic analysis. In any case, Bull got his own back in a 1967 review of Schelling's *Arms and Influence*. On the eve of his arrival as The Australian National University's second Professor of International Relations, Bull wrote:

> This book does not add any major ideas to the stock of very remarkable ones that are contained in Thomas Schelling's writings. But it brings the old ideas together in a more or less orderly exposition: it spells some of them out more fully; it detaches some of them from the framework of the general theory of conflict and places them in the context of an analysis of international relations; and it demonstrates that the author has been reading some translations of the classics.[53]

That last judgement may have been aimed at Schelling's citation of Xenophon's account of the Persian Expedition:[54] far from being a long-term influence on his earlier theory, Schelling told me he in an interview that he had simply found the translation in an airport bookstand.

Schelling would himself publish an influential volume in 1961 on the same subject. This was *Strategy and Arms Control* [55] which Schelling co-authored with Morton Halperin. Along with Bull's book and a collection edited by Donald G. Brennan,[56] also published in 1961, these formed the trio of arms control classics for the nuclear age. Schelling and Halperin saw their work as being less concerned with the broader political context of arms control. They advertised their work as concentrating on the 'military environment' rather than the 'more purely political and psychological consequences'[57] of arms control. Indeed in an interview I conducted in 1996, Schelling told me that they had made a deliberate decision to exclude political considerations so as to emphasise the military element. To some extent this may have been a matter of brand differentiation; after all, they had access to an early draft of Bull's book while writing their own text. But it also reflected Schelling's theoretical predisposition as a microeconomist to use parsimonious models of strategic behaviour which assume away broader contextual factors.

Stanley Hoffman explains the distinction by stating that Bull's

> work on arms control ... was planted firmly in a political context, unlike, for instance, the contribution of Thomas Schelling. Like Schelling, Hedley Bull emphasised the unity of strategic doctrine and of arms control; unlike him, Bull also believed in the unity of all military policies (whether strategic or arms control) and foreign policy.[58]

One of Schelling's most vivid phrases is 'the diplomacy of violence',[59] by which he means the informal and tacit but powerful messages which the use of armed force can deliver. Bull spent a good deal of his time appreciating the broader political and diplomatic context in which those messages might be transmitted.

This early 1960s connection between Bull and Schelling suggests a mutual respect between the two authors, and also a degree of competition in their approach. But what can it tell us about the title of this paper—their common interest in common interest? One sign of a connection in this regard comes in Bull's discussion mid-way through *The Control of the Arms Race* of explicit arms control agreements between the powers. Cautioning against the belief in disarmament agreements as a solution to the competition for military advantage, he writes that

> an agreement, if it is reached, represents not the discovery of the solution to a problem, but *the striking of a bargain*. As in other kinds of bargaining agreements may emerge when proposals are worked out that advance the interests of both without injuring the interests of either.[60]

There are no footnotes to this section, but the italicised phrase 'the striking of a bargain' and the reference to other kinds of bargaining which advance both sides interests without harming either one of them is, in my opinion, close to pure Schelling.

For Schelling, strategy was all about bargaining situations. The ability to strike bargains was the secret to stable strategic relations. In *The Strategy of Conflict*, he writes:

> A bargain is struck when somebody makes a final, sufficient concession.
> ... There is some range of alternative outcomes in which any point is
> better for both sides than no agreement at all. To insist on any such point
> is pure bargaining, since one always would take less rather than reach
> no agreement at all, and since one always can recede if retreat proves
> necessary to agreement.[61]

This encapsulates the two points evident in Bull's comment about arms control agreements: that they involve the striking of a bargain, and that they represent a common interest between parties who might otherwise harm one another's interests if they are not able to agree.

Rather than Bull's emphasis on explicit and formal arms control agreements, Schelling's argument deals more with implicit or tacit bargains—where the parties somehow coordinate informally their behaviour around focal points which stand out from the background like the 38th parallel in Korea. Bull certainly has an interest in the informal arrangements which can produce order in the absence of formal government. In a conversation I was able to have in 2007 when she was visiting Australia, Mary Bull noted her late husband's interest in tacit agreements and in Schelling's work in this area. But Hedley Bull was, at least by 1967, not so sure about tacit agreements. He writes

> that there are such agreements, that they play a very important part in
> the structure of international relationships, and that Schelling has done
> a great service by opening up this question, is beyond dispute. ... But
> he has done nothing to produce by way of evidence except speculations.
> I find it hard to recognise American and Soviet behaviour in his picture
> of two governments orchestrated by purposive individuals, sending and
> receiving messages and ironing out understandings in these ... fields
> with scarcely as much as a nod or a wink.[62]

This is not to imply that Bull regarded Schelling's general contribution as wanting. In one of his most prominent essays published a year earlier, Bull argued that Schelling

> has contributed as much as and perhaps more than any other thinker of
> the scientific genre to the theory of international relations. His elaboration
> of the notion of arms control, the elements of deterrence, the nature of
> bargaining, the place in international relations of threats of force are of
> a rare originality and importance and will probably prove to have a
> lasting impression on the theory and, indeed, the practice of these
> matters.[63]

My analysis of this Bull–Schelling connection may seem a little strained. After all, a good deal of the inspiration for Schelling's argument about the striking of bargains by parties due to their common interest in avoiding mutual harm is associated from his non-zero-sum reformulation of game theory. Such formal and potentially pseudo-scientific treatments of international behaviour held little water for one of the founders of the English school of international relations who railed against false quantification. The immediately previous quotation praising Schelling comes from his essay 'International Relations: The Case for a Classical Approach', in which Bull made some fairly swingeing attacks on those who would view international politics as a science reducible to experimentally testable hypotheses.[64]

But Schelling was a very unorthodox game theorist, interested not in the artificial production of numerical answers to qualitative problems, but in the powerful ideas which game theory helped isolate—including the interdependence of adversaries' behaviour and interests. And in a 1972 essay, which ended up in *Australian Outlook*—the precursor to today's *Australian Journal of International Affairs*—and which began as a paper read to an Australian National University Department of International Relations seminar, Bull points out that some of the formal theorists were more than worth paying attention to. Recalling the piece he had written some six years earlier, Bull writes:

> I also make it clear that some of the theorists whose work I classified as 'scientific' have made major contributions to the study of international relations. I have, for example, heaped high praise on Morton Kaplan and Karl Deutsch [two of the founders of the systems approach to international relations].

And then he goes straight on:

> while Thomas Schelling I consider to be one of the major thinkers of the era, one of the few figures to have worked in international relations whose ideas have penetrated far beyond the subject to become part of the general intellectual culture of the age.

In concluding this assessment, Bull nails the informality of Schelling's formal theorising by saying: 'My argument was that "scientific" theorists who had made significant contributions did so by failing to adhere to their own methodological principles and reverting to the "classical" style of argument.'[65] Indeed in an earlier essay he had observed very shrewdly that 'a number of strategists, like Thomas Schelling who have mastered this technique, but in their work exercises in game theory serve only to illustrate points that are independently arrived at'.[66]

Bull's comments could not have been more apt in terms of Schelling's own scholarship. What Bull saw as admirable as a classical theorist was objectionable to the gatekeepers of the formal game theory. When Schelling's *Strategy of Conflict* was reviewed by leading game theorist Martin Shubik, the following criticism resulted:

> It is my opinion that this book would have been a much stronger contribution had most of the references to game theory been deleted. Although the formal structure of the topic could have been of considerable assistance to the type of analysis presented by Schelling, there is little evidence that it has been used.[67]

Schelling's work was also criticised for similar formal inadequacies by Oskar Morgenstern[68] (one of game theory's giants), who wrote a few years later that 'the theory of games is a mathematical discipline designed to treat rigorously the question of optimal behavior of participants in games of strategy and to determine the resulting equilibria'.[69] Rather interestingly, Bull observed in 1968 that, 'as far as I know, the only person who has claimed that game theory presents a method of solving strategic problems is Oskar Morgenstern of Princeton University'.[70] It is quite clear that Bull regarded himself on Schelling's side of the game theory debate. Not only did he reject the more quantitative approach, he also evidently had little time for the claims that Schelling's adaptation of game theory to strategic thinking was dangerous, calling Anatol Rapoport's work 'wrong-headed but subtle and powerful'.[71]

A Common Interest in Pure Cooperation?

Bull and Schelling drew strength from a shared realisation that informal collaboration between the great powers, or the nuclear-armed superpowers, was possible in the absence of an overarching sovereign. An international version of Hobbes' leviathan was not necessary. This collaboration was possible because the great powers were interrelated by common interest as well as competitive interest: they could limit the latter (according to Bull if they so chose as responsible heirs of the European international society and according to Schelling if they appreciated the nuclear predicament which made cooperation a requirement for survival).

But there is also a sense in both scholars' writings that the common interest can be extended much further towards situations of purer cooperation where the competitive element in international politics is almost obscured. In Schelling's work, this approach is evident in *The Strategy of Conflict* where he draws on theories of pure coordination where social units need to maximise their collaboration to emerge with a common focus or pattern.[72] This encourages a potentially hazardous optimism. For example, Schelling regarded the limits being observed by US action in Vietnam in the mid-1960s as an important case of strategic bargaining, where those limits were being clearly communicated to North Vietnam.[73] But the likelihood of success relied on Schelling's universalistic assumption that Hanoi was motivated by common as well as competitive interests. North Vietnam's political interests turned out to be much more zero-sum than he perhaps realised, and the moderating impact of nuclear weapons upon state ambitions did not extend as far as he had thought.

Schelling has been criticised for an approach which encourages the exploitation of violence in international affairs and risks making the world a more dangerous and violent place.[74] But here he emerges as rather too optimistic about the possibilities of strategic cooperation and the limitation of violence, and possibly exaggerates the extent of common interest between strategic actors. Yet it is this sort of logic which helps explain the award of the Nobel Prize, and the appeal of his work beyond strategic studies into sociology and theories of international regimes.

Bull's contemporaneous work from the early 1960s can hardly be accused of excessive optimism. *The Control of the Arms Race* in particular resembles a demolition job on the arguments for international disarmament and leaves little room for notions of unrelenting international progress. Schelling catches this atmosphere well, noting in his review that he agreed with John Strachey that the book 'offers only wisdom and perspective rather than bright hopes'.[75] It is noticeable that strategic studies academics, whose subject displaces economics as the true dismal science, seem drawn to the noticeably pessimistic refrain in Bull's work of the 1960s which also infected good parts of *The Anarchical Society*.

But, as some scholars have observed, the so-called 'later Bull' seemed to allow more scope for what he called the 'solidarist' interpretation of international society where the interests of the whole international community would increasingly dominate the plural interests of individual states. This theme is evident in Bull's early work. It is certainly there in *The Anarchical Society*: Alderson and Hurrell note that one of the readers of the manuscript described the work as 'hopelessly over-optimistic'.[76] By the early 1980s, some of Bull's work may even risk echoing the Kantian arguments he rejected earlier on. For example, his arguments for the just treatment of 'third world' countries within the international system, and to 'some degree of commitment to the cause of individual human rights on a world scale'[77] seem some distance from the brilliant grumpiness of his earlier writings, partially infused as these were with the melancholy of power politics. This increasing cosmopolitan streak may help explain why Bull has been claimed by some scholars as an early constructivist.[78] The appeal here is not just because this later work might be read to imply the primacy of evolving social norms over hard power, but also because the evolution of Bull's own thinking might be read as an example of the social construction of ideas.

Of course, this also means that in Bull's work in particular there is something for just about everyone. It is just possible that a baby bear, mama bear and papa bear would all find parts of his work to their liking, or at least tasty enough to require a response. The same is true for strategists, for members of the English School—both explicit and tacit, for positivist and post-positivist international relations scholars, and also for those who belong to more than one of these categories. This is why it is especially apt that so many of us will be inhabiting the Hedley Bull Centre.

ENDNOTES

[1] This chapter is based on a paper read to the Strategic and Defence Studies Centre seminar series, The Australian National University, August 2007.

[2] Hedley Bull, 'Strategic Studies and Its Critics', *World Politics*, vol. 20, no. 4, July 1968, pp. 593–605.

[3] Revelation 3:16, *The Bible*, New International Version translation.

[4] Hedley Bull, *The Anarchical Society: A Study of Order in World Politics*, Macmillan, Basingstoke, 1977, pp. 26–27. On the consistent importance of common interests in Bull's view of international relations, see Kai Alderson and Andrew Hurrell, 'Bull's Conception of International Society', in Alderson and Hurrell (eds), *Hedley Bull on International Society*, Macmillan, Basingstoke, 2000, p. 5.

[5] Hedley Bull, comments to the British Committee on the Theory of International Politics (Sunday afternoon, 15 April 1962, 2.30 pm–4.30 pm) in Alderson and Hurrell, *Hedley Bull on International Society*, pp. 119–20.

[6] Thomas C. Schelling, *The Strategy of Conflict*, Harvard University Press, Cambridge, MA, 1960, pp. 14–15.

[7] See Robert Ayson, *Thomas Schelling and the Nuclear Age: Strategy as Social Science*, Frank Cass, London, 2004, pp. 54–57.

[8] Schelling, *The Strategy of Conflict*, p. 5.

[9] Bull, *The Anarchical Society: A Study of Order in World Politics*, p. 59.

[10] See R.J. Vincent, 'Order in International Politics', in J.D.B. Miller and R.J. Vincent (eds), *Order and Violence: Hedley Bull and International Relations*, Clarendon Press, Oxford, 1990, p. 38. Also see Alderson and Hurrell, 'Bull's Conception of International Society', p. 3.

[11] Alderson and Hurrell, 'Bull's Conception of International Society', pp. 5–6.

[12] See J.D.B. Miller, 'Hedley Bull, 1932–1985', in Miller and Vincent (eds), *Order and Violence: Hedley Bull and International Relations*, pp. 4–5.

[13] Bull, *The Anarchical Society: A Study of Order in World Politics*, p. 16.

[14] Hedley Bull, 'The Grotian Conception of International Society', in Herbert Butterfield and Martin Wight (eds), *Diplomatic Investigations: Essays on the Theory of International Politics*, Allen & Unwin, London, 1966, pp. 70–71.

[15] Bull, 'The Grotian Conception of International Society', pp. 65 and 67.

[16] Kai Alderson and Andrew Hurrell, 'International Society and the Academic Study of International Relations', in Alderson and Hurrell (eds), *Hedley Bull on International Society*, pp. 27–28.

[17] Hedley Bull, 'International Theory: The Case for a Classical Approach', *World Politics*, vol. 18, no. 3, April 1966, p. 375.

[18] See Thomas Schelling, 'Prospectus for a Reorientation of Game Theory', RAND P-1491, 17 September 1958, p. 121. For Sherif's work, see Muzafer Sherif, *The Psychology of Social Norms*, Harper, New York, 1936.

[19] For an example of Schelling's comments on learning, see Schelling, *The Strategy of Conflict*, p. 168.

[20] ee Alderson and Hurrell, 'International Society and the Academic Study of International Relations', p. 27.

[21] See the analysis in Ayson, *Thomas Schelling and the Nuclear Age*, pp. 93-99.

[22] Bull, *The Anarchical Society: A Study of Order in World Politics*, p. 184.

[23] Bull, *The Anarchical Society: A Study of Order in World Politics*, p. 188.

[24] Thomas C. Schelling, 'International Cost-Sharing Agreements', in *Essays in International Finance*, No. 24, International Finance Section, Department of Economics and Sociology, Princeton University, Princeton, September 1955.

[25] Bull, *The Anarchical Society: A Study of Order in World Politics*, p. 4. For a recent commentary, see John Williams, 'Order and Society', in Richard Little and John Williams (eds), *The Anarchical Society in a Globalized World*, Palgrave Macmillan, Basingstoke, 2006, p. 18.

[26] Bull, *The Anarchical Society: A Study of Order in World Politics*, p. 3.

[27] Bull, *The Anarchical Society: A Study of Order in World Politics*, p. 27.

[28] Stanley Hoffman, 'International Society' in Miller and Vincent (eds), *Order and Violence: Hedley Bull and International Relations*, p. 19.

[29] See Herbert Butterfield, 'The Balance of Power', in Butterfield and Wight (eds), *Diplomatic Investigations: Essays on the Theory of International Politics*, p. 132.

[30] Schelling, *The Strategy of Conflict*, p. 4.

[31] See Anatol Rapoport, *Strategy and Conscience*, Harper & Row, New York, 1964; and Philip Green, *Deadly Logic: The Theory of Nuclear Deterrence*, Ohio State University Press, Columbus, 1966.

[32] See Hoffman, 'International Society', p. 32.

[33] James L. Richardson, 'The Academic Study of International Relations', in Miller and Vincent (eds), *Order and Violence: Hedley Bull and International Relations*, p. 153.

[34] Hedley Bull, *The Control of the Arms Race*, Weidenfeld & Nicolson for the Institute of Strategic Studies, London, 1961, p. 48. (And quoted in Hoffman, 'International Society', p. 32).

[35] Bull, 'International Relations as an Academic Pursuit', (1972) in Alderson and Hurrell, *Hedley Bull on International Society*, p. 259.

[36] Hedley Bull, review of *Arms and Influence* by Thomas C. Schelling, *Bulletin of the Atomic Scientists*, March 1967, pp. 25–26.

[37] Hoffman, 'International Society', p. 15.

[38] See Thomas C. Schelling, 'War Without Pain and Other Models', review of *Conflict and Defence: A General Theory* by Kenneth E. Boulding, *World Politics*, vol. 15, no. 3, April 1963, p. 473.

[39] Hence the titles of his later books, Thomas C. Schelling, *Micromotives and Macrobehavior*, W.W. Norton, New York, 1978; and Thomas C. Schelling, *Choice and Consequence*, Harvard University Press, Cambridge, MA, 1984.

[40] See Bull, *The Anarchical Society: A Study of Order in World Politics*, p. 202. For discussion and criticism of this approach, see Richard Little, 'The Balance of Power and Great Power Management', in Little and Williams (eds), *The Anarchical Society in a Globalized World*, pp. 110–11.

[41] See Thomas C. Schelling, *Arms and Influence*, Yale University Press, New Haven and London, 1966, p. 87n5.

[42] Schelling, *Arms and Influence*, p. 33.

[43] Schelling, *The Strategy of Conflict*, p. 239.

[44] Bull, *The Control of the Arms Race*, p. 60.

[45] Bull, *The Control of the Arms Race*, p. 60 n. 17.

[46] As recorded in J.D.B. Miller, 'Hedley Bull, 1932–1985', p. 6.

[47] See Robert O'Neill and David N. Schwartz (eds), *Hedley Bull on Arms Control*, Macmillan, Basingstoke, 1987, p. 3.

[48] See Hedley Bull, 'Disarmament and the International System', (1959), in O'Neill and Schwartz (eds), *Hedley Bull on Arms Control*, pp. 27–40.

[49] Thomas C. Schelling, review of *The Control of the Arms Race* by Hedley Bull, *Survival*, vol. 3, no. 4, July–August 1961, p. 195.

[50] Thomas C. Schelling, review of *The Control of the Arms Race*, p. 195.

[51] Thomas C. Schelling, review of *The Control of the Arms Race*, p. 196.

[52] O'Neill and Schwartz, 'Introduction', in O'Neill and Schwartz (eds), *Hedley Bull on Arms Control*, p. 1.

[53] Hedley Bull, review of *Arms and Influence* by Thomas C. Schelling, *Bulletin of the Atomic Scientists*, March 1967, p. 25.

[54] Thomas C. Schelling, *Arms and Influence*, pp. 12–13.

[55] Thomas C. Schelling and Morton H. Halperin, *Strategy and Arms Control*, The Twentieth Century Fund, New York, 1961.

[56] See Donald G. Brennan (ed.), *Arms Control, Disarmament, and National Security*, George Braziller, New York, 1961.

[57] Schelling and Halperin, *Strategy and Arms Control*, p. 6.

[58] Hoffman, 'International Society', p. 31.

[59] This is the title of the first chapter of Schelling, *Arms and Influence*, pp. 1–34.

[60] Bull, *The Control of the Arms Race*, p. 69.

[61] Schelling, *The Strategy of Conflict*, pp. 21–22.

[62] Bull, review of *Arms and Influence*, p. 26.

[63] Hedley Bull, 'International Theory: The Case for a Classical Approach', *World Politics*, vol. 18, no. 3, April 1966, p. 368.

[64] See Bull, 'International Theory: The Case for a Classical Approach', pp. 361–67.

[65] Bull, 'International Relations as an Academic Pursuit' p. 256.

[66] Bull, 'Strategic Studies and its Critics', pp. 601–602. On Bull's admiration for what one especially perceptive scholar calls the 'tacit use of the classical approach' in the work of Schelling and Kaplan, see Richardson, 'The Academic Study of International Relations', p. 170.

[67] Martin Shubik, review of *The Strategy of Conflict* by Thomas C. Schelling and *Fights, Games and Debates* by Anatol Rapoport, *Journal of Political Economy*, vol. 64, no. 5, October 1961, p. 502.

[68] See Oskar Morgenstern, review of *Fights, Games and Debates* by Anatol Rapoport and *The Strategy of Conflict* by Thomas C. Schelling, *Southern Economic Journal*, vol. 28, no. 1, July 1961, pp. 103–105.

[69] Oskar Morgenstern, 'Game Theory: Theoretical Aspects', in *International Encyclopedia of the Social Sciences*, Macmillan and the Free Press, New York, 1968, vol VI, p. 62.

[70] Bull, 'Strategic Studies and its Critics', p. 602.

[71] Bull, 'Strategic Studies and its Critics', p. 601.

[72] See Schelling, *The Strategy of Conflict*, p. 85.

[73] See Schelling, *Arms and Influence*, p. 171.

[74] See Richard Ned Lebow, 'Thomas Schelling and Strategic Bargaining', *International Journal*, vol. 51, no. 3, Summer 1996, pp. 555–76.

[75] Schelling, review of *The Control of the Arms Race*, p. 196.

[76] Alderson and Hurrell, 'Bull's Conception of International Society', p. 15.

[77] Hedley Bull, 'Justice in International Relations: The 1983 Hagey Lectures', in Alderson and Hurrell, *Hedley Bull on International Society*, pp. 221–22.

[78] As noted in Alderson and Hurrell, 'International Society and the Academic Study of International Relations', pp. 34–35.

Chapter 6

Hedley in Canberra

Bruce Miller

I

The story of Hedley's coming to Canberra begins, in a sense, one day in 1951, when, in the quadrangle at the University of Sydney, I was accosted by a young man in a well-fitting suit who said his name was Hedley Bull. He said that he and some of his friends (he was specialising in Philosophy and History) had decided to form a Sydney University Political Science Association, and would like me to be President. I explained that I was a Staff Tutor in the university's adult education department and so not a member of the intra-mural staff; but he pointed out that there was no Political Science department (the nearest was Public Administration in the Faculty of Economics) and, in effect, I would have to do.

I saw quite a bit of him in the subsequent year, before I left to study at the London School of Economics (LSE). It was clear that he was bright, charming and a genuine seeker after knowledge. His study under John Anderson had equipped him with a properly sceptical disposition, which was endorsed by his life-long immersion in History. I think you could call us friends.

After I got to London I lost track of him; he was in Oxford and busy there. It was not until 1955, when I left the LSE to go to Leicester University, that I took up with him again. Charles Manning, the Professor of International Relations at the LSE, had made me an Assistant Lecturer the previous year, largely because I had no previous training in the subject, and he wanted his staff to listen only to him. When I left he appointed Hedley in my place, for much the same reason. Otherwise Hedley would have gone off to Aberdeen University to teach Political Philosophy. The job at the LSE was the start of his rise.

II

Now I can cut forward to 1961–62. This is when I was recruited by Sir John Crawford, recently appointed as Director of the Research School of Pacific Studies, to be Professor of International Relations. When appointed, he had required that International Relations should be returned to his Research School after a period in the Political Science department in the Research School of Social Sciences, following a chaotic and confused life subject to major disturbances.[1]

Crawford's account of the state of the department was not encouraging. Its few members had been given the choice to stay with Political Science or come to Pacific Studies, and the brightest and the one acquainted with current American Scholarship, Arthur Burns, had elected to stay. Only George Modelski had a training in international relations. There needed to be an expansion.

My thoughts soon turned to Hedley. While I was at Leicester, he had gone from strength to strength. Martin Wight and Alastair Buchan had taken him to their hearts, Manning approved, he had had an American debut, and he was clearly the man of the future in British International Relations. Crawford told me that there was a Professorial Fellowship available if I could find a suitable candidate. I told Hedley I would nominate him for it if he wanted to come back to Australia.

He said he wanted to do so eventually, but it was too soon. He had a lot to do in London. So the job went to Modelski, but my eyes were still on Hedley.

So they remained until I went on study leave in London in late 1965. Hedley had meanwhile been made head of the Arms Control and Disarmament Research Unit in the Foreign Office, while retaining his Readership at the LSE. We met for lunch one cold day, and I told him that I was prepared to arrange with Crawford for a second chair in the Department, with joint headship, provided it went to Hedley if his references were satisfactory. (Crawford told me afterwards that he had never seen such impressive references anywhere.) I told Hedley that I was pretty sure my demand would be accepted by The Australian National University, and that no future time would be so ripe. After consideration, he said yes, and on returning to Canberra I set the machinery in motion. It worked, and in June 1967 he and the family arrived.

III

So far as I know, The Australian National University had no previous experience of a joint headship, and there were those of the god–professors who said it would not work. In fact it did.

The system was that we would each do two years as head, turn and turn about, subject to each other's study leave absences. In those days Research School professors had every fourth year away. When we were both in Canberra, we consulted on all major questions: only once in the ten years do I remember our disagreeing, and I soon knew that he was right and I was wrong. We had identical rooms across from the department's small office, and it was easy to be constantly in touch. As my colleagues and I soon knew, his judgment was very sound.

When he came, the department was in better shape than it had been five years before. We were still in an era of major Commonwealth government spending for The Australian National University, and our School had been among the beneficiaries. Crawford had been generous, and I think he felt that the money had been mostly well spent. The staff was bigger and more professional. There was, however, an underlying feeling in the Research School that we were not doing enough research in the regional area, particularly in Southeast Asia.

From the start, my opinion about this had been that international relations as a feature of the world affairs was too great to be contained within a program which concentrated on a particular geographical area. Whatever, the superpowers did affect other states, including all those in our region, however that might be defined. We were then the only International Relations department in any Australian university. It was our duty, where possible, to make our students aware of the many conflicting currents of international politics, so that when they went out to teach in other universities, they would be better equipped than as regional specialists.

Hedley fully agreed. Indeed, he aided the process. He brought to the department a more international focus than it had previously been possible to give it. His own recognition in Britain and the United States ensured this, as did his own previous work. He made the bipolar aspect of the world situation, with all its implications, plainer to all.

It was emphasised by at least two things during his time in Canberra. One was his own study leaves—one at Columbia University in New York, one at Jawaharlal University in New Delhi, and one at All Souls, Oxford. His contacts on these occasions provided us with new staff in one case and a variety of Visiting Fellows as well. There were also some from his time in London, the most notable of whom was Adam Watson, a former diplomat who shared with him the editorship of later books.

However, in looking for Hedley's influence while in Canberra, one must take full note of his influence on students—all post-graduate and all on scholarships. Here he was as successful and as effective as he had been in London and was later to be in Oxford. He was prepared to take pains and time to provide the criticism and encouragement which any student needs who is proceeding towards a PhD. He took a personal interest in each one, as they would all now acknowledge. John Vincent and Des Ball gave him special pleasure.

His influence was not confined to those for whom he was supervisor. Each week the department had a seminar, which all staff and students were expected to attend. One of us would write a paper on his or her current concerns, and cyclostyled copies of this would be distributed to all in advance. At the seminar the author would speak to the substance of the paper, and then there would be general discussion.

The benefit was not only to students, but also to staff, whose papers would not only benefit from criticism, but also provide material for later publication, not least, *The Anarchical Society: A Study of Order in World Politics*. Hedley acknowledged this in his own case, but also saw what advantage the rest of us gained from it. That gain, again and again, would come from his analysis of the paper, to which he had given close attention, and his suggestions for improvement. He was receptive to all criticism, and rarely showed that ferocity which some scholars, especially Americans, had experienced at conferences. He was a mentor of the highest order.

Hedley's sense of the importance of students was manifest in his advocacy of an MA course as a possible precursor of any embarcation on the PhD. Here his and my awareness of the American system came into play. He was worried to find that the students to whom we awarded scholarships at the end of their BA course had rarely, if ever, done any work in international relations. They had usually done history or economics. The few Americans whom we attracted were exceptions, but few meant few.

Hedley's wish was that we would institute an MA degree by coursework which would provide scholarships in advance of PhD work. I agreed. There were two obstacles. One was that the Research Schools had provided scholarships only for the PhD, the other was that the MA had been the domain of the Faculty of Arts and obtained only by a dissertation.

It took much time and trouble before we could get our MA established in 1975. We could not make it a mandatory requirement for the PhD, but it soon took off in its own right as The Australian National University's second Master's degree by coursework. Now the university is awash with them.

IV

To turn to Hedley's Canberra activities beyond the simple confines of the department's teaching and supervision is to enter something of a contested sphere. As the only department of the subject in the university system, our staff were often called upon to help with other efforts at international understanding, to comment on current affairs, and occasionally to provide expertise, or at least suggestion, to government, though that did not always prove popular.

Two offshoots of the department in which Hedley was involved were the Strategic and Defence Studies Centre and the Third Monday Group. Once again, these were cases of Crawford's foresight and generosity in accepting advice. The first of them was modelled in some degree on the Institute of War and Peace Studies at Columbia University (headed by Professor William J.K. Fox, who, together with his wife Anne, was later a valued Visiting Fellow). The purpose of the Centre was to provide what Australian universities had not previously had—a place at which major questions of defence policy could be discussed from the standpoints of scholars rather than those of partisans, which in public had normally been the case. It developed effectively with the leadership firstly of Tom Millar and then of Bob O'Neill, both of them members of the department.

This was certain to be something of interest to Hedley, given his activities in London and at the International Institute of Strategic Studies (IISS). It was very much to his credit that he attempted no take-over bid. We did have some problems involving which of the institutions—Centre and Department—might claim funds from the School's total, but these were easily resolved. The Centre went on to be a major factor in any debate on Australian defence policy, and on our place in the world. Hedley had been far-sighted in supporting it.

The Third Monday Group was the product of a period before my own arrival in Canberra, when a group of academics from The Australian National University (not from the department, but some in the Research School) had attacked the Southeast Asian Treaty Organisation (a 'paper tiger' now forgotten) and the award of an honorary degree to the King of Thailand. It seemed to me that this had created a situation in which public servants no longer talked to academics (if they had ever done so in any measure), contrary to what I had experienced in London and New York.

I constructed a dining club consisting of half academics and half senior public servants in those fields concerned with external relations—Defence, Foreign Affairs, Immigration, Trade and Treasury—and put the proposition to Crawford in the first instance, and then with his support to Arthur Tange. It worked. With these two major figures in Public Service eyes, it lasted for ten years, month by month, a talk from either side of the table—or, increasingly, from the person next to you—followed by a vigorous discussion. When a new Minister for Defence appeared, we asked him along too.

Hedley fitted in as by nature to this environment. He was an Australian academic, he had worked in the Foreign Office, he was fully aware of the importance of officials in formulating policy, and he proved to be an acceptable interlocutor to all those he met. Like our other departmental members of the Group, he found the senior officials easy to deal with, and perhaps more able than ignorant academics had previously thought. Hedley managed the Group when I was away, and I am sure he enjoyed it.

He came a bit closer to political publicity when in November 1972 he signed, along with Keith Hancock, Walter Crocker (who had been the first professor in the department), Manning Clark and others, a letter to the papers denouncing the McMahon Government's performance, especially in foreign policy, and advocating a vote for Labor—which won the subsequent election.

This was an unusual excursion into party politics for Hedley, who did not think of himself as a party man. It was motivated by the absurdities of McMahon, especially, I think, by that nonsensical fellow's approach to China. Most of us were rather pleased.

He took a keen interest in the Australian Institute of International Affairs, being its Research Director from 1968 to 1973. He gave lectures at a number of other Australian universities, thus enlarging the department's reach, and spoke often at various international conferences and at universities overseas. He was, in fact, an academic celebrity; not so much in the glamour sense, but that of being recognised as a leader in thinking and writing about the subject.

His connection with the IISS remained close; he acted as Australian representative on its Council, and was later very much a factor in the appointment as its Director of Bob O'Neill, one of our own people.

It is difficult for me to recognise just what was his overall effect on the Australian academic and political system, because he meant so much to me personally. But it is clear that he was a looming presence, someone who elicited admiration, even envy at times, for the effortless way in which he went about his work, and the efficiency of all he did. I have mentioned elsewhere his methods with a manuscript. He did not type, but wrote in a small but highly legible hand right up to the left edge of the page. When asked to provide a margin for comments and corrections he would politely decline. What he wrote he stood by because he had worked it out fully in advance. This did not mean he was averse to criticism, only that this could wait until the paper or chapter was complete. It was always a masterful piece.

Yet he was really masterful in personal relations. This was a man happily playing pat-ball tennis with me on Saturday mornings, who sent his children postcards adorned with funny drawings when he was abroad, who came into my room one day with an atlas, saying he couldn't find Barataria. I set him right, but have only recently found that there is a Gulf of Barataria somewhere in the West Indies; it would have been a help to know this at the time.

He was thus a complete man: masterful when necessary, humane and even sentimental when out of the firing line. We owe him so much. The Australian National University is right to commemorate him with the opening of the Hedley Bull Centre.

ENDNOTES

[1] See S.G. Foster and Margaret M. Varghese, *The Making of the Australian National University 1946–1996*, Allen and Unwin 1996, pp. 108–109 and pp. 132–33 for a full treatment.

Chapter 7

Conversations with Hedley

Adam Watson

When I first got to know Hedley Bull, he was a political theorist, interested especially in the international models of systems of states.[1]

He accepted that any group of states, so involved with each other that each had to take account of all the others, could be called a system. When such states consciously developed, and in the main observed certain rules, and operated certain common institutions, and perhaps shared some values (though shared values were not essential), they could be considered to have formed an international society.

Martin Wight proposed in meetings of the British Committee on International Theory that where every state in a system recognised the same degree of independence for all the other members as it claimed for itself, we could call it an international system; but where a few big states had rights and responsibilities that others did not—whether *de jure* or *de facto*—we should speak of hegemonial or suzerain systems. Wight and I agreed about the substantial degree of hegemony in the European states system and in the worldwide system which grew out of it. I maintained that, in practice, every known 'international' system had some degree of hegemony, and that the concept of a wholly anarchical society of states was a theoretical absolute that had never been realised.

Hedley Bull, in conversations with me, agreed about the prevalence of some degree of hegemony or imperial authority in historical practice. He said he was not a historian but a political scientist. His point was that, nonetheless, this concept of a society of fully independent and juridically equal states did exist, and that it played a large part for several centuries in European thought about international relations, and also to some extent their conduct in practice. In particular, the heady era of Western decolonisation in which we were then living was dominated by the ideal of a non-hegemonial world society of independent states, to which all remaining colonies ought to accede forthwith regardless of their competence. Hedley, as an Australian, regarded the attainment by dependent states of full independence as a natural evolution towards an almost unquestionable goal. Hedley, of course, recognised that dependent states might become integral and equal parts of an extended imperial power, as the French, Portuguese and Soviets for instance, proposed.

So it was possible for Hedley, and many others, to regard the propensity to hegemony, which I saw as an integral and ever-present feature of systems of substantially independent states, as an aberration or defect, a failure so far to achieve the more perfect society towards which we were moving. Wight distrusted this belief in Progress. He once observed in this context that to err is human—that is, if hegemony was a failure to achieve perfection, it was a permanent failure. But in spite of Hedley's theoretical assumptions, he became, like me, increasingly interested in hegemonial and suzerain systems, and accepted the metaphor of a spectrum from anarchy to empire—from a state of nature to a single universal leviathan.

Hedley Bull's great book, *The Anarchical Society*, is about the ideal international society and progress towards it. It does not even dismiss hegemony as an aberration, and its index does not include the word. This seemed to him a reasonable limitation for one book. But he was steadily becoming more interested in the historical record—'la storia' itself as Herbert Butterfield liked to call it. He thus came to see the key role of hegemony and anti-hegemonial coalitions in international practice. Understanding and analysing this side of the story was to be my job, and he encouraged me to write about it.

Hedley came to see the origins of the anarchical ideal in the Westphalian settlement of 1648 and the anti-hegemonial coalition that established it. He studied the historical record of that settlement carefully and in detail. In so doing, he saw increasingly how much the realities of seventeenth century European history differed from what is now often called the Westphalian ideal. But the ideal continued over the centuries to influence practice in many ways. For instance, a main purpose of the rules and institutions of the European international society, from *cujus regio ejus religio* to the United Nations, and especially the operation of the balance of powers, was in Arnold H.L. Heeren's classic phrase 'to protect the weak against the strong'. The goal of a free anarchical world of multiple independences, made up largely of emancipated colonies, most notably the United States, effectively relegates hegemony and even more suzerainty from endemic conditions to the very obstacles to be overcome. Or so it seemed to most of us in the 1960s and 1970s. It is my impression that Hedley, especially as he became more historically minded, did not fall into this trap.

Hedley Bull saw that the states which regained their independence from European domination, or acquired it for the first time, accepted the general structure of the worldwide society of states: though it was of Western origin it appeared to the rulers of the new states capable of serving their needs. But otherwise the 'third world' that had been assigned subordinate or colonial status by the expansion of the European society of states, seemed to Hedley determined to reject Europe. He intended to write a companion volume to *The Expansion of*

International Society, to be called *The Revolt against the West*, which would show Asia, Africa, Latin America and Oceania as rejecting not only Euro/North American political, administrative and economic standards, but also the West's cultural standards and practices.

In our discussion of this projected volume, I urged him to include the rejection of the Soviet Union by those Communist states which were independent enough to do so. Thus, of the four major founders of the non-aligned movement, two—Nehru and Nasser—were opposed to British imperialism, and the two others—Zhou Enlai and Josip Tito—opposed Soviet domination. But we both realised that we did not know enough about the Communist side of the equation to write about it; and of course our discussions took place before Mikhail Gorbachev and the collapse of Soviet domination.

Hedley seemed to me always somewhat uneasy about the relationship of the newly independent non-white world to Western values and standards of civilisation. To many Westerners in the 1960s and 1970s, the decolonisation movement and the adoption of universally valid standards of human rights, democracy, the position of women in society, the protection of the environment and so on, went hand in hand.

Hedley personally favoured these values as much as any member of the British Committee, including myself. But his understanding of the international situation was that the world was moving towards a society of some 200 substantially independent and therefore culturally very diverse states. The symbolism of the United Nations was the principle of universal membership. Acceptance of a state into the United Nations legitimised membership of international society, and therefore legitimised cultural diversity—a worldwide version of *cujus regio ejus religio*.

The international scene has greatly changed since Hedley Bull and I had these discussions. We thought in terms of a global society where we co-existed, and to some extent collaborated with Communists and ayatollahs as well as still primitive communities. We did not foresee the collapse in our working lifetimes of bipolarity, or the great technological and military predominance of the United States. But, notwithstanding these changes, the Westphalian ideal and Westphalian assumptions remain vigorous and widespread. Most significantly, the long-term assumptions of the United States about a desirable world order remain Westphalian, rooted in its war of independence. And even if the ideal of multiple and therefore diverse independences turns out to be only a crock of fairy gold at the end of the Westphalian rainbow, still *The Anarchical Society*, and Hedley Bull's work generally, will retain their definitive value in formulating and analysing the concept of a Westphalian world.

More generally, it is well to remember that all ideas do not have the same force. The 'unalienable right to life, liberty and the pursuit of happiness' and 'liberté, égalité, fraternité' have been *idées notrices* of world political history since their proclamation. And in the more limited sphere of relations between states, the same seems to be true of the Westphalian ideal that Hedley Bull set himself to define.

ENDNOTES

[1] With minor alteration, this chapter was originally published as 'Recollection of my discussions with Hedley Bull about the place in the history of International Relations of the idea of the Anarchical Society' by Adam Watson, Paris, July 2002, available at <http://www.leeds.ac.uk/polis/englishschool/watson-bull02.doc>, accessed 16 June 2008.

Chapter 8

Hedley in his Own Words: three essays

What follows are three essays written by Hedley Bull. The first essay, 'Order vs. Justice in International Society', appeared in the journal *Political Studies* (vol. xix, no. 3, September 1971, pp. 269–83). The paper was originally delivered to the Annual Conference of the Political Studies Association at Birmingham on March 1971.

The second essay, 'Martin Wight and the Theory of International Relations: The Second Martin Wight Memorial Lecture', appeared in the *British Journal of International Studies* (vol. 2, 1976, pp. 101–106). The original lecture for this paper was delivered on 29 January 1976 at the London School of Economics.

The final essay 'The Revolt against the West' appeared in *The Expansion of International Society* (eds Hedley Bull and Adam Watson), Oxford University Press, Oxford, 1984.

The three essays are reprinted here with the kind permission of Wiley-Blackwell Publishing, Cambridge University Press, and Oxford University Press respectively.

(1) Order vs Justice in International Society

Order is not merely an actual or possible condition or state of affairs in world politics, it is also very generally regarded as a value. But it is not the only value in relation to which international conduct can be shaped, nor necessarily an overriding one. At the present time, for example, it is often said that whereas the Western powers, in the justifications they offer of their policies, show themselves to be primarily concerned with order the states of the so-called Third World are concerned with the achievement of justice in the world community, even at the price of disorder. Professor Ali Mazrui, one of the few contemporary writers on international relations to have thought deeply about this question, has said that the Western powers, the principal authors of the United Nations Charter, wrote it in such a way that peace and security are treated as the primary objectives of the organisation, and the promotion of human rights as a secondary objective, whereas the African and Asian states are dedicated to reversing this order of priority.[1]

Whether or not Professor Mazrui is correct in characterising in this way the conflicts of policy between the Western powers and the African and Asian states is a matter on which a good deal might be said. My purpose in what follows, however, is not to enter into this question but to consider in general what order and justice are in world politics and how they are related to one another. In particular, how far are 'order' and 'justice' (in various of the meanings that may be assigned to these terms) compatible or mutually re-inforcing ends of policy and how far are they conflicting or even mutually exclusive? To the extent that 'order' and 'justice' do stand in opposition to one another what is to be made of the view that in international life the former has always had or should have priority over the latter? To make sense of these questions we must first pay attention to the meaning of the terms.

II

To say of a number of things that together they display order is (in the simplest and most general sense of the term) to say that they are related to one another according to some pattern, that their relationship is not purely haphazard but contains some discernible principle. Thus a row of books on a shelf displays order whereas a heap of books on the floor does not. But when we speak of order in social life what we have in mind is not *any* pattern or principle in the relations among individuals or groups, but a pattern that produces a particular result or facilitates the achievement of a particular purpose. Order in this purposive sense is displayed by a row of books that are not merely placed together on a shelf but arranged in alphabetical order so as to facilitate the object of finding a book by a particular author. Augustine defined the term in this relational or purposive way: he spoke of order as 'a *good* disposition of discrepant parts, each in its *fittest* place' (my italics).[2]

'Good' or 'fittest' for what? A disposition or pattern of social relations that is good for one purpose will not be good for another. What was 'order' in France in this sense for the court of' Louis XVI was not for the Jacobins, what is 'order' in the world today in this sense for the United States is not for China or Cuba or North Vietnam. The term 'order' like the term 'stability' is in fact often used in this way in the West today to refer to patterns or dispositions of international or domestic political relations that embody the preferred values of the West.

Our present concern, however, is not to state what is the preferred order of the West or of some other group of powers but to define social order as such, order as opposed to disorder, order that will be found to exist both in the France of the *ancien régime* and in post-revolutionary France, both in an American-preferred world order and in a Soviet-preferred or Chinese-preferred one. By order in social life I mean a pattern or structure of human relationships that sustains not the special purposes of this or that sort of society but the primary or elementary goals of social coexistence; goals that are common to social life at all times and in all places. Social life in any form requires, for example, some restriction on the liberty of members of the society to resort to violence, a presumption that promises will be kept; and a means of securing stability of possession.

International order is a pattern or structure of human relations such as to sustain the elementary or primary goals of social coexistence among states. A number of independent political communities might in principle exist without forming together an international *system* in the sense that they are related to one another as a set of interacting parts, as indeed the independent political communities of pre-Columbian America did not form an international system together with those that existed in Europe. When a number of independent political communities do together comprise an international system they do not necessarily constitute an international *society* in the sense that they conceive themselves to be bound by a common set of rules in their relations with each other and to share in the working of a common set of institutions. Turkey, Japan and China, for example, were part of the European-dominated international system before they were in the full sense part of the European-dominated international society. That is to say, they interacted significantly with European powers in war and commerce before they and the European powers came to regard each other as subject to the same set of rules and as cooperating in the operation of common institutions.

The element of international order that exists in the world reflects the fact that sovereign states today constitute, however precariously, an international society as well as an international system. It is difficult to conceive of international order apart from norms or rules: in particular, elementary or primary rules requiring states to limit the violence they bring to bear on one another, to honour undertakings and to respect one another's spheres of jurisdiction. It is true that some of the most important sources of international order are the consequence simply of certain brute facts about the international system that would make for international order even if what I have called international society did not exist: the fact, for example, that military power is distributed in such a way that no one state is preponderant; the fact of the fear of war; the fact of economic inter-dependence. But while these facts provide a basis for the perception by states of common interests in international order, actually to achieve it they must be able to arrive at guidelines or signposts that show them how they must behave if they are to advance these common interests: that is to say, they must articulate norms or rules and agree upon them.

These rules are prior to international law, international morality and international institutions; they may have the status simply of operating procedures or 'rules of the game'. Their existence in some form is a necessary condition of what I have called an international system, as well as of an international society: it is difficult to conceive that sustained military or commercial intercourse could be carried on between independent political communities, without some degree of expectation of conformity to general imperative principles of conduct, however crudely and tentatively formulated. But these rules of the game are strengthened if they are embodied in institutions, as some of them have been in the institutions of modern international society: international law, the diplomatic system, the principle that there should exist a balance of power and acceptance of the special managerial role of the great powers.

It may be helpful to indicate the relationship between international order, in the sense in which it has been defined, and a number of different although connected concepts. If *international* order pertains to the elementary conditions of social coexistence among states *world* order may be thought of as the patterns of behaviour that sustain elementary social coexistence among mankind as a whole. In the present phase of universal political organisation, the dominant feature of which is the division of mankind and of the earth's surface into separate sovereign jurisdictions, world order may be thought of as the sum of domestic order and international order, the order that is provided within states and the order that exists among them. But of course world order could in principle be achieved by other forms of universal political organisation, and a standing question is whether it does not require other forms.

International order is closely related to what in the language of the UN Charter is called 'peace and security'. It has often been pointed out that peace and security do not necessarily belong together: while in the circumstances of the Soviet–American strategic stalemate there exist both peace and a degree of security, at the time of Munich there was peace in Europe but not security, while at the time of the San Francisco Conference there was security but not peace. The coupling of the two terms together in the Charter reflects the judgements that the requirements of security may conflict with those of peace, and that in this event the latter will not necessarily take priority.

International order cannot be identified with peace in the sense of the absence of war because achievement of the minimum goals of coexistence between states may be found to require the use or threat of force. Nor can international order be identified with security, which may be defined as safety from war and military defeat. The provision of a degree of security or safety from violent attack is one, but only one of the basic goals of international coexistence, which must be taken also to refer to the acceptance by states of one another's rights to a sphere jurisdiction and to engage in peaceful intercourse.

International order is sometimes defined (e.g. by Quincy Wright) in terms of the predictability of future international behaviour.[3] As I have defined it, order in international relations bears a close relationship to predictability but should not be identified with it. If there is international order, then to the extent the statesmen understand what the patterns are that sustain coexistence, a consequence will be that some basis for prediction will exist. Moreover, the desire to be able to predict the behaviour of other states, to avoid the anxiety into which we would be plunged if we could not count on others to follow certain guidelines or signposts, helps to explain why it is that we regard international order as valuable. But order is not the same as predictability for there are patterns or regularities of international behaviour, of which we may be aware and from which we may form expectations about the future, which are in fact patterns of disorder or anarchy: the breakdown of restraints on international violence, the disregard of established undertakings and the infringement of sovereign jurisdiction may occur in a regular and predictable way but international order, as I have argued, is not any pattern or regularity but a pattern of a particular sort.

It is obvious that in taking international order to concern the primary or elementary conditions of international coexistence I am concerning myself with what is sometimes called *minimum* order rather than with *optimum* order, with what, for example, Myres S. MacDougal calls 'minimum world public order' rather than with the more inclusive 'world public order with human dignity'.[4] The question I am trying to raise here is how 'minimum international order' is related to 'optimum international order', to a framework of international relations that provides for other values besides that of 'order'.

III

Unlike order, justice is a term which can ultimately be given only some kind of private or subjective definition. I do not propose to set out any private vision of what just conduct in world politics would be, nor to embark upon any philosophical analysis of the criteria for recognising it. My starting-point is simply that there are certain ideas or beliefs as to what justice requires in world politics and that demands formulated in the name of these ideas play a large role in the course of events.

Clearly, ideas about justice belong to the class of moral ideas, ideas which treat certain human actions as right in themselves and not merely as a means to an end, as categorically and not merely hypothetically imperative. Considerations of justice, accordingly, are to be distinguished from considerations of law, and from considerations of the dictates of prudence, interest or necessity.

In thinking about justice there are certain familiar distinctions which it is helpful to bear in mind.[5] First, we may distinguish what has been called 'general' justice, justice as identical with virtuous or righteous conduct from 'particular' justice, justice as one species of right conduct among others. The term 'justice' is sometimes used interchangeably with 'morality' or 'virtue', as if to say an action is just were simply another way of saying that it is morally right. It is often argued, however, that ideas about justice constitute a particular subcategory of moral ideas, as we imply when we say that justice should be tempered with mercy, or that independent political communities in their dealings with one another are capable of justice but not of charity. It has often been contended that justice is especially to do with equality in the enjoyment of rights and privileges, perhaps also to do with fairness or reciprocity; that whatever the substance of the rights or privileges in question demands for justice are demands for the equal enjoyment of them as between persons who are different from one another in some respect but should be treated in respect of these rights as if they were the same.

Demands for justice in world politics are often of this form: they are demands for the removal of privilege or discrimination, for equality in the distribution or in the application of rights as between the strong and the weak, the large and the small, the rich and the poor, the black and the white or the victors and the vanquished. It is important to distinguish between 'justice' in this special sense of equality of rights or privileges and 'justice' in the wider sense in which we are using it interchangeably with 'morality'. The question needs to be raised whether justice in this larger sense will always be satisfied by equality of rights, whether it does not sometimes require discrimination between great powers and small, Have states and Have Nots, nuclear and non-nuclear, and so on.

Justice may be held to lie in the recognition of certain specified rights or duties—political, social or economic—but the demand for justice in the sense of the equal enjoyment of rights or equal imposition of duties for like individuals and groups is heard irrespective of what the substance of the rights and duties is. Thus another important distinction is between 'substantive' and 'formal' justice, the former lying in the recognition of specified rights or duties and the latter in like application of them to like persons. Demands for 'equality before the law', demands that legal rules be applied in a like manner to like classes of people, are an example of demands for 'formal justice' in this sense, but the latter arise in relation to all rules, legal or non-legal. When Britain and France attacked Egypt in 1956 and President Eisenhower insisted that the duty of member states of the United Nations to refrain from the use or threat of force except in self-defence applied to the allies of the United States as well as to others, he was demanding 'formal justice' in this sense.

Equality may be envisaged as the enjoyment by a like class of persons or groups of *the same* rights or duties. But it is obvious that equality in this sense will often fail to satisfy other criteria of justice. For one thing, given that persons and groups are sometimes unequal in their capacities or in their needs, a rule that provides them with the same rights and duties will have the effect simply of further underlining their inequality: as Aristotle wrote, 'injustice arises when equals are treated unequally and also when unequals are treated equally'.[6] Thus the distinction is sometimes drawn between 'arithmetical justice' in the sense of equal rights and duties, and 'proportionate justice' in the sense of rights and duties that are distributed proportionately to the object in view. Marx's principle 'from each according to his capacity, to each according to his need' embodies a preference for 'proportionate' justice over 'arithmetical' in relation to the distribution of wealth. In world politics certain basic rights and duties, such as the right of sovereign jurisdiction and the duty of non-intervention, generally held to apply equally to all states, exemplify 'arithmetical justice', while the doctrine that the use of force in war or reprisals should be in proportion to the injury suffered, may be taken illustrate 'proportionate justice'.

Another distinction, closely connected with the latter, is between 'commutative' or reciprocal justice, and 'distributive' justice or justice assessed in the light of the common good or common interest of society as a whole. 'Commutative justice lies in the recognition of rights and duties by a process of exchange or bargaining, whereby one individual or group recognises the rights of others in return for their recognition of its own. To the extent that the bargaining strength of the individuals or groups concerned is equal, this reciprocal process is likely to result in what we have called 'arithmetical justice' or the same rights. 'Distributive justice', by contrast, comes about not through a process of bargaining among individual members of the society in question, but by decision of the society as whole, in the light of consideration of its common good or common interest. It is clear that 'distributive justice' in this sense may often take the form of justice which is 'proportionate' rather than 'arithmetical', requiring, for example, that the rich pay higher taxes than the poor.

To the extent that world politics is principally a process of conflict and cooperation among states having only the most rudimentary sense of the interests of the world as a whole, it is the domain pre-eminently of ideas of 'commutative' justice rather than 'distributive'. The main stuff of contention about justice in international affairs is to be found in the attempt of sovereign states, through a process of claim and counter-claim, to iron out among themselves what rights and duties will be recognised and how they will be applied. But ideas of 'distributive' justice, I shall try to show, have also come to play a significant part in the discussion of justice in world politics, if not yet to be prime movers of events.

Finally, it is important to consider in what agents or actors in world politics moral rights or duties are taken to be vested. Here one may distinguish what may be called interstate or international justice, individual or human justice, and cosmopolitan or world justice.

By interstate or international justice I have in mind the moral rules held to confer rights and duties upon states and nations, e.g. the idea that all states, irrespective of their size or their racial composition or their ideological leaning, are equally entitled to the rights of sovereignty, or the idea that all nations are equally entitled to the right of self-determination. The rights of states and of nations may, of course, conflict with one another. The principle of national self-determination has been invoked to destroy the sovereign integrity of states and even now threatens a great many of them; but to the extent that there is now a broad consensus that states should be nation-states and that the official doctrine of nearly all states is that they are nation states, there is a measure of harmony between the ideas of interstate justice and international justice.

By individual or human justice I mean the moral rules conferring rights and duties upon individual human beings. In the form of the doctrines of natural law and natural rights, ideas of human justice historically preceded the development of ideas of interstate or international justice and provided perhaps the principal intellectual foundation upon which these latter ideas at first rested. That is to say, states and nations were originally thought to have rights and duties because individual persons had rights and duties, the rulers of states being persons and nations being collections of persons. But the ideas of interstate and international justice by the eighteenth century reached a point of take-off, after which they became independent of the means by which they had become established as rights and duties were held to attach to the notional personality of a state which was other than its rulers and the collective personality of a nation which was other than, and on some views more than, the sum of its members.

In this system in which rights and duties applied directly to states and nations, the notion of human rights and duties has survived but it has gone underground. Far from providing the basis from which international justice or morality is derived it has become potentially subversive of international society itself, a position reflected in the classical doctrine of international law that states are the only subjects of international law and that individuals are merely the objects of understandings between states, The basic compact of coexistence between states, expressed in the exchange of recognition of sovereign jurisdictions, implies a conspiracy of silence entered into by governments about the rights and duties of their respective citizens. This conspiracy is mitigated by the practice of granting rights of asylum to foreign political refugees, by declaratory recognition of the moral rights of human beings in such documents as the Atlantic Charter, the U.N. Charter and the Universal Declaration of Human Rights, and by practical cooperation between governments to take account of human rights in such fields as the treatment of prisoners of war and the promotion of economic and social welfare. But the idea of the duties of the individual human being raises, in international politics, the question of the duties he has that conflict with his duties to the state—the question that the Nuremberg War Crimes Tribunal raised in relation to German soldiers and political leaders, and which as Judge Telford Taylor has pointed out, they have raised also in relation to the American soldiers and leaders responsible for the prosecution of the Vietnam War.[7] And the idea of the rights of the individual human being raises in international politics the question of the right and duty of persons and groups other than the state to which he owes allegiance to come to his aid in the event that his rights are being disregarded—the right of the Western powers to protect the political rights of the citizens of eastern European countries, of Africans to protect the rights of black South Africans, of Australians or New Guineans to protect the rights of Indonesian citizens in West Irian. These are questions which, answered in a certain way, lead to disorder in international relations or even to the breakdown of international society itself.

In addition to ideas about interstate or international justice, and about human justice we need to recognise a third category of ideas which concern what may be called cosmopolitan or world justice. These are ideas which seek to spell out what is just or right or good for the world as a whole, for an imagined *civitas maxima* or cosmopolitan society to which all individuals belong and to which their interests should be subordinate. One thinks, for example, of Kenneth Boulding's attempt to spell out the idea of a world economic interest, of C. Wilfred Jenks' notion of an emergent common law of mankind that will replace law between states, and of much of the presently fashionable discussion of the global or cosmic problem of man and the environment.[8] This notion of justice as the promotion of the world common good is different from that of the assertion of the rights and duties of individual human beings all over the globe for it posits the idea that these individuals form or should form a society or community whose common interests or common good must qualify or even determine what their individual rights and duties are, just as the rights and duties of individuals within the state have in the past been qualified or determined by notions such as the common good, the greatest happiness of the greatest number or the general will. It calls for distributive rather than purely commutative justice.

These notions of world or cosmopolitan justice are at present inchoate and of slight practical importance. The world society or community whose common good they purport to define does not exist except as an idea or myth which may one day attract enough followers to become of practical importance, but has not done so yet. Political mankind as such does not have the means of interest articulation and aggregation, of political recruitment and socialisation which, we are told, are the hallmarks of a political system. Insofar as the interests of mankind at large are articulated and aggregated, this is through the mechanisms of the society of sovereign states. For authoritative guidance as to what the interests of the world as a whole might be with regard, for example, to the distribution of economic resources, or the control and distribution of population, or the conservation of the environment, we can only look to the views of sovereign states and of the international organisations which they dominate. There is, indeed, no lack of self-appointed spokesmen of the common good of 'the spaceship earth' or 'this endangered planet', and indeed there are non-governmental international bodies with valid claims to express the ideas of transnational groups of various kinds. But the views which these private individuals and bodies express are not the outcome of any political process of the assertion and reconciliation of interests; they provide indeed less in the way of an authoritative guide to the interests of the world as a whole than do the views of sovereign states, even unrepresentative or tyrannical ones, which are at least the authentic expression of the perceived interests of some part of the globe. But if it is chiefly through the views of states that we must seek to discover the world common good, this is bound to be a distorting lens; universal ideologies that are espoused by states are notoriously subservient to their special interests, and agreements reached among states notoriously the product of bargaining and compromise rather than of any consideration of the interest of the population of the countries they represent treated as a whole.

IV

How are order and justice in world politics related to one another? There are some who would say that there is little or nothing of either and therefore no basis for pursuing the question. But the two things whose relationship I wish to consider are quite concrete. On the one hand there are the institutions and mechanisms whereby international society does provide a framework of international order or minimum coexistence. On the other hand there are the ideas or beliefs about justice in world politics that I have outlined. To what extent does the framework of international order satisfy the various aspirations for justice that are prevalent in the world? And what would be the effects on international order of the attempt to realise their aspirations or to realise them more fully?

It is obvious that the existing framework of international order fails to satisfy some of the most deeply felt and powerfully supported of these aspirations for justice. It is true that justice in any of its forms is realisable only in a context of order, and that international society, by providing this context, may be regarded as paving the way for the equal enjoyment of rights of various kinds. It is true that international society as such, through such nearly universal organs as the United Nations and its Specialised Agencies is formally committed to much more than the preservation of minimum order or coexistence: it espouses ideas of interstate and international justice, and of individual or human justice, although perhaps not of world justice; and it facilitates intergovernmental cooperation in many fields to promote the realisation of these ideas.

But, to begin with, the framework of international order is quite inhospitable to projects for the realisation of cosmopolitan or world justice. If the idea of the world common good were to be taken seriously, it would lead to the consideration of such questions as how the immigration policies of states throughout the world should be shaped in the general interest, which countries or which areas of the world have the most need of capital and which the least, how trade and fiscal policies throughout the world should be regulated in accordance with a common set of priorities, or what outcomes of a host of violent civil and international conflicts throughout the world best conformed to the general interests of mankind.

These are of course the very issues over which governments have control and do not seem likely to be willing to relinquish control in the absence of vast changes in human society. The position which governments occupy as custodians of the perceived interests of limited sections of mankind imposes familiar obstacles to their viewing themselves simply as so many agencies jointly responsible for the implementation of the world common good. It is sometimes said that the commitment of the donor countries through aid and trade policies to the objective of a minimum level of economic welfare throughout the world implies and presupposes acceptance of the idea of the interests of the community of mankind. Kenneth Boulding, for example, argues that since the transfer of resources from rich countries to poor is wholly one-sided or non-reciprocal it means that the rich see themselves as part of the same community with the poor. 'If A gives B something without expecting anything in return, the inference must be drawn that B is 'part' of A, or that A and B together are part of a larger system of interests and organisations.'[9] It is not clear, however, that the idea of the community of mankind does actually underlie the enterprise of the transfer of resources to any important degree; or indeed that the transfer of resources yet has a secure and established position as part of the permanent business of international society, assailed as it is on the one side by the idea that the rich countries should reduce their involvement in the Third World to the minimum, and on the other side by the doctrine that aid is essentially a means of perpetuating domination and exploitation and hence prejudicial to the true interests of the Have Nots.

The framework of international order is inhospitable also to demands for human justice, which unlike projects for cosmopolitan or world justice represent a very powerful ingredient in world politics at the present time: in the form, for example, of the demands of poor countries for economic justice for their inhabitants or the demands of African states for racial justice in southern Africa. International society takes account of the notion of human rights and duties that may be asserted against the state to which particular human beings belong but it is inhibited from giving effect to them, except selectively and in a distorted way. If international society were really to treat human justice as primary and coexistence as secondary, if, as Professor Mazrui says the African and Asian states want, the UN Charter were to give pride of place to human rights rather than to the preservation of peace and security, then in a situation in which there is no agreement as to what human rights are or in what hierarchy of priorities they should be arranged, the result could only be to undermine international order and, incidentally, such prospects as there might be for justice as well. It is here that the society of states—including, I should say, despite what Professor

Mazrui says, African and Asian states—display their conviction that international order is prior to human justice. African and Asian states, like other states, are willing to subordinate order to human justice in particular cases closely affecting them, but they are no more willing than the Western states or the states of the Soviet bloc to allow the whole structure of international coexistence to be brought to the ground.

There is another obstacle to the realisation of human justice within the present framework of international order. When questions of human justice achieve a prominent place on the agenda of world political discussion, it is because it is the policy of particular states to raise them. The world heard about the war guilt of the Kaiser and later witnessed the trial and punishment of German and Japanese leaders and soldiers by international procedures for war crimes and crimes against the peace. It did not witness the trial and punishment of Allied leaders and soldiers who *prima facie* might have been as much or as little guilty of disregarding their human obligations as Göring, Yamamoto and the rest. This is not to say that the idea of the trial and punishment of war criminals by international procedure is unjust or unwise, only that it operates in a selective way. That these men and not others were brought to trial by the victors was an accident of power politics.

In the same way the world has heard of the human rights of non-European persons in southern Africa, and may even come to see redress of the wrongs they have suffered, because it is the policy of black African states to take up this issue, just as the world once heard of the rights of the Christian subjects of the Sultan of Turkey because it was the policy of Gladstonian England to uphold them. But the rights of Africans in black African states, or of intellectuals in the Soviet Union, or of Tibetans in China or Nagas in India or communists in Indonesia are less likely to be upheld by international action because it is not the policy of any prominent group of states that they should be. The international order does not provide any general protection of human rights, only a selective protection that is determined not by the merits of the case but by the vagaries of international politics.

There is a further obstacle. Even in cases where, as the consequence of these vagaries of international politics, international society permits action directed towards the realisation of human justice, the action taken does not directly impinge upon individual human beings but takes place through the mediation of sovereign states, who shape this action to their own purposes. Take the case of world economic justice, towards the realisation of which the transfer of resources from the rich countries to the poor is bent. The ultimate moral object of this process is to improve the material standard of life of individual human beings in poor Asian, African and Latin American countries. But the donor countries and international organisations concerned transfer resources not directly to these individuals but to the governments of the countries of which they are citizens. As Julius Stone points out, it is left to these governments to determine the criteria according to which the resources will be distributed to individuals, or indeed to distribute them arbitrarily or not distribute them at all. As he says, the unspoken assumption of the business of transfer of resources is that the actual claimants and beneficiaries of what he calls the 'justice constituency' are not individual human beings but governments.[10] The doubts which donor countries entertain about the way in which the governments of recipient countries distribute or fail to distribute the resources transferred to them of course constitute one of the principal disincentives to foreign aid. Yet one has also to agree with Stone's conclusion that although the transfer of resources, as it takes place at present, necessarily falls short of the realisation of what I have called human justice, it is not possible, given the present nature of international society, for it to take place in any other way: donor countries and organisations cannot determine in detail the way in which recipient governments distribute resources transferred to them so as to realise notions of cosmopolitan justice without violating the most fundamental norms of the compact of coexistence.

If international society is quite inhospitable to notions of cosmopolitan justice and able to give only a selective and ambiguous welcome to ideas of human justice, it is not basically unfriendly to notions of interstate or international justice. The structure of international coexistence, as I have argued, itself depends on norms or rules conferring rights and duties upon states—not necessarily moral rules, but procedural rules or rules of the game which in modern international society are stated in international law. These rights and duties which states have, moreover, they have to an equal degree, as Emer de Vattel pointed out in his celebrated argument that equality is a corollary of sovereignty: 'A dwarf is as much a man as a giant is, a small republic no less a sovereign state than the most powerful kingdom.' Whereas ideas of world justice may seem entirely at odds with the structure of international society and notions of human justice to entail a possible threat to its foundations, ideas of interstate and international justice may reinforce the compact of coexistence between states by adding a moral imperative to the imperatives of enlightened self-interest and of law by which it is defined.

Yet international order is preserved by means which systematically affront the most basic and widely agreed principles of international justice. I do not mean simply that at the present time there are states and nations which complain that they are denied their rights, and perhaps are denied their rights, as Laos and Cambodia are denied their rights of sovereignty or Kashmir or Quebec or Tibet is denied its right of self-determination. It is the normal condition of any society that some of its members should feel that their rights are infringed. What I have in mind is that the institutions and mechanisms that sustain international order, even when they are working properly, indeed especially when they are working properly or fulfilling their functions, necessarily violate ordinary notions of justice.

Consider, for example, international law. It is not merely that international law sanctifies the status quo without providing for a legislative process whereby the law can be altered by consent and thus causes the pressures for change to consolidate behind demands that the law should be violated in the name of justice. It is also that when the law is violated, and a new situation is brought about by the triumph not necessarily of justice but of force, international law accepts this new situation as legitimate, and concurs in the means whereby it has been brought about. As Mazrui writes, international law condemns aggression, but once aggression has been successful it ceases to be condemned. The conflict between international law and notions of international justice is endemic because the situations from which the law takes its point of departure are a series of *faits accomplis* brought about by force and the threat of force, legitimised by the principle (distinguishing international law from municipal) that treaties concluded under duress are valid. *Ex factis jus oritur.*

Moreover, contrary to much superficial thinking on this subject, it is not as if this tendency of international law to accommodate itself to power politics were some unfortunate but remediable defect that is fit to be removed by the good work of some high-minded professor of international law or by some ingenious report of the International Law Commission. There is every reason to think that this feature of international law, which sets it at loggerheads with elementary notions of justice, is vital to its working; and that if international law ceased to have this feature, it could not play any role at all.

Or consider the role that is played in the maintenance of international order by the special position of the great powers. Great powers contribute to international order by maintaining local systems of hegemony within which order is imposed from above, and by collaborating to maintain the global balance of power and, from time to time, to impose their joint will on others. But the great powers, when they perform these services to international order, do so at the price of systematic injustice to the rights of smaller states and nations, the injustice which is felt by states which fall within the Soviet hegemony in eastern Europe or the American hegemony in the Caribbean, the injustice which is written into the terms of the UN Charter which prescribe a system of collective security that cannot be operated against great powers.

Consider again the role that is played in international order by the 'balance of terror' or relationship of mutual deterrence between the superpowers, or the wider historical role of the institution of the balance of power, of which the former is in some respects a variant. Here is an institution which offends against ordinary and widely agreed notions of international justice and also human justice, in ways that need not be elaborated here, and yet whose role in the preservation of international order at the present time is a central one.

V

Given that the framework of international society fails to satisfy these various ideas of justice that have been considered, what would be the effects upon international order of attempts to realise them? Can justice in world politics, in its various senses, be achieved only by jeopardising international order? And if this is so, which should take priority?

It is possible to distinguish three ideal types of doctrines which embody answers to these questions. There is first the conservative or orthodox view that recognises an inherent conflict between the values of order and of justice in world politics, and treats the former as having priority over the latter—international society as a society in which 'minimum order' or coexistence is the most that can be expected, and in which demands for a just or 'optimum order' threaten to remove the small area of consensus upon which this coexistence is built.

There is secondly the view of the revolutionary which also is founded upon the idea of an inherent conflict between the present framework of international order and the achievement of justice, but treats the latter as the commanding value: let justice be done 'though the earth perish'. The revolutionary, however, does not believe that the earth will perish, only that the damned will perish: the saved may look forward to the re-establishment of an order that will secure the just changes he wishes to bring about, after a period of temporary and perhaps geographically limited disorder. This has been the doctrine of some black Africans in relation to the African continent, or Arab nationalists in relation to the Arab lands, and of the early Bolsheviks and now of China in relation to the world as a whole.

Thirdly, there is the liberal or progressivist view that has always represented one important strand in thought about foreign policy in the West, that (perhaps without denying it altogether) is reluctant to accept that there is any necessary conflict between order and justice in world politics, and is constantly seeking after ways of reconciling the one with the other. It is inclined, for example, to see the righting of injustices as the true means to the strengthening of international order: the removal of *apartheid* or of 'the last vestiges of colonialism' as the way in which the black African states can best be integrated into the system of 'peace and security', the provision of economic justice for the poor peoples of the world as the means of avoiding an otherwise inevitable violent confrontation of Haves and Have Nots. It is inclined to shy away from the recognition that justice in some cases can be brought about only by violent change, to cling to the idea that just change may be brought about through processes of consent or consensus, to argue that attempts to achieve justice by disrupting order are counter-productive, to cajole the advocates of 'order' and of 'justice' into remaining within the bounds of a single moral system that provides for both and permits an adjustment that can be mutually agreed.

It is clear that where the states concerned are willing to give their *consent* to a change brought about in the name of an agreed notion of justice (as when India demanded for herself and Britain conceded the right of national self-determination) this may take place without prejudice to the foundations of international order. It is clear also that even where there is not consent by all the parties affected, but there is overwhelming evidence of a *consensus* in international society as a whole in favour of a change held to be just (especially if the consensus embraces all the great powers) the change may take place without causing other than a local and temporary disorder, after which the international order as a whole may emerge unscathed or even appear in a stronger position than before. The action taken by Britain, on the authority of the Congress of Vienna, to suppress the slave trade, fell into this category.

The conflict between international order and demands for justice arises in those cases where there is no consensus, or no sufficiently overwhelming consensus, as to what justice involves, when to press the claims of justice is to reopen questions which the compact of coexistence requires to be treated as closed. If there were a consensus within the United Nations, including all the great powers, in favour of military intervention in Southern Africa to enforce national self-determination for black majority populations and to uphold black African political rights, it might be possible to regard such intervention as implying no threat to international order, or even as strengthening international order by confirming a new degree of moral solidarity in international society. In the absence of such a consensus, demands for external military intervention imply the subordination of order to considerations of international and human justice. The argument that has been advanced by black African states in the Security Council since 1963 to the effect that *apartheid* is not merely a violation of human rights but a threat to the peace, whatever merits it may or may not have as a construction of the law of the Charter or as a political tactic, obscures the position: it is the proponents of intervention who wish to threaten the peace, and they are moved by considerations not of peace but of justice.

The military action taken by India against Portugal in 1961 and by Indonesia in West Irian in 1962 also represented the breaking of the peace for the sake of change conceived to be just. It is interesting that in these cases, as in relation to proposed military intervention in southern Africa, the justifications provided related to order as well as to justice, Krishna Menon defending India's action in terms of the need to respond to Portugal's aggression of 1510 (since when there had been 'permanent aggression'), as well as in terms of India's right to conduct a just war of national liberation. Thus the revolutionaries accommodate themselves to the prevailing modalities of the system.

When then, demands for justice are put forward in the absence of a consensus within international society as what justice involves, the prospect is opened up that the consensus that does exist about order or minimum coexistence will be undone. The question has then to be faced whether order or justice should have priority.

It would not make sense to argue that one or the other value should always have priority in any given case. In fact, ideas of both order and justice enter into the value systems, the justificatory or rhetorical stock-in-trade of all actors in world politics. The advocate of revolutionary justice looks forward to the time when a new order will consolidate the moral gains of the revolution. The proponent of order takes up his position partly because the existing order is, from his point of view, morally satisfactory, or not so unsatisfactory as to warrant its disturbance. The question of order vs. justice will always be considered by the parties concerned in relation to the merits of a particular case.

When the merits of any particular case are considered, moreover, the priority of order over justice cannot be asserted without some assessment of the question whether or not or to what extent injustice is embodied in the existing order. Why do we regard order as valuable? As Mazrui writes, 'the importance of peace is, in the ultimate analysis, *derivative*. Taken to its deepest human roots peace is important because "the dignity and worth of the human person" are important'.[11] Those who are unwilling to jeopardise international order for the sake of anti-colonial or racial or economic justice reach their conclusions because of the assessments they make about justice as well as order, whether the former are acknowledged or not.

When all these qualifications have been made, it may still be contended that international order is prior to justice—international, human or cosmopolitan—in the sense that it comprises the elementary or primary conditions of international coexistence, which have to be satisfied at least in some measure before justice in any of its senses can be realised. It cannot be concluded from this, however, that the preservation of international order should be preferred to the realisation of justice in any particular case; and to the extent that the framework of international order is a strong one, it is able to withstand the shock of violent assaults carried out in the name of justice. The nuclear peace, in particular, has made the world safe for just wars of national liberation, carried out at the sub-nuclear level, and the international or interstate peace has made the world safe for just internal or civil violence.

(2) Martin Wight and the Theory of International Relations: The Second Martin Wight Memorial Lecture

There is no lecture which I could feel more honoured to have been asked to give than one which commemorates the name of Martin Wight. Just twenty years ago I made the same journey I have just made—from Oxford to the London School of Economics—to take up a position as assistant lecturer in the Department of International Relations. I had not done a course of any kind in International Relations, nor made any serious study of it, and as I arrived in Houghton Street I wondered how I was to go about teaching the subject and even whether it existed at all.

It was Professor Manning who urged me to attend the lectures on International Theory being given by Martin Wight, then reader in the Department. These lectures made a profound impression on me, as they did on all who heard them. Ever since that time I have felt in the shadow of Martin Wight's thought—humbled by it, a constant borrower from it, always hoping to transcend it but never able to escape from it. Until 1961, when he moved to the University of Sussex, I was his junior colleague. After that time I was able to keep in touch with his work through the meetings of the British Committee on the Theory of International Politics, for which many of his best papers were written and about which Sir Herbert Butterfield, who originally convened the Committee, spoke in his lecture inaugurating this series.[12] Since Martin Wight's death in 1972 I have become more intimately acquainted with his ideas than ever before, through being involved in the editing of his unpublished manuscripts.

Let me say a little about this. Wight was a perfectionist who published very little of his work. His writings on International Relations comprise one sixty-eight page pamphlet, published thirty years ago by Chatham House for one shilling and long out of print, and half a dozen chapters in books and articles, some of the latter placed in obscure journals as if in the hope that no one would notice them. He was one of those scholars—today, alas, so rare—who (to use a phrase of Albert Wohlstetter's) believe in a high ratio of thought to publication.

It has seemed to me a task of great importance to bring more of his work to the light of day. The task would be impossible but for the encouragement and constant help I have received from two people to whom I should like to pay tribute: Martin's wife Gabriele and his pupil and friend Harry Pitt of Worcester College, Oxford. That the work he left should be published at all was not self-evident. Some of the work is unfinished. Some may never have been intended for publication. If it was his judgement that the work did not meet the very high standards he set himself for publication, should his judgement not be respected? For myself, what has weighed most is not the desire to add lustre to Martin Wight's name, but my belief in the importance of the material itself and in the need to make it available to others, so that the lines of inquiry he opened up can be taken further. Especially, perhaps, there is a need to make Martin Wight's ideas more widely available in their original form, rather than through the second hand accounts of others, such as myself, who have been influenced by him.

It is my hope that two and possibly three publications by Martin Wight will in due course appear. The first is a series of essays on different aspects of the modern states system and of other historical states systems, which he wrote in the last eight years of his life for meetings of the British Committee. The second is a revised and much expanded version of *Power Politics*, the Chatham House essay of 1946 to which I referred a moment ago, the completion of which—unhappily, he did not complete it—he saw as his principal scholarly task.[13] In preparing this manuscript I have been fortunate in securing the cooperation, as co-editor, of Carsten Holbraad, who was Martin Wight's student both at the London School of Economics and at Sussex, and in recent years has been a colleague of mine in Canberra. Thirdly, I hope that it will be possible in some form to make available to others the lectures on International Theory which impressed me so deeply when I arrived at the London School of Economics and are at once the least published and the most profound of his contributions to International Relations. Fortunately the notes of these lectures—detailed and immaculate in his beautiful handwriting—have been preserved.

I propose to devote this lecture to a discussion of some of Martin Wight's own ideas. I shall not attempt to provide a survey of his life and thought as a whole. Such a survey—I have sought to provide the sketch of one in the introduction to one of the forthcoming volumes—would have to deal not only with his ideas about international Relations but also with his ideas about the philosophy of history, about education and about Christian theology. It would have to take account of his close association with Arnold Toynbee, with whom he worked at Chatham House both on *A Study of History* and on the *Survey of International Affairs*, and from whom he derived his commitment to universal history and his interest in the relationship between secular history and what he called sacred history or divine providence. Mention would have to be made of the influence upon him as a very young man of Dick Sheppard, the Vicar of St Martin's-in-the-Field and a founder of the Peace Pledge Union, and of his conversion in the late 1930s to Christian pacifism, a position to which he adhered steadfastly throughout that apparently most just of wars, Britain's struggle in the Second World War. One would have to consider the books he wrote, while a member of Margery Perham's team at Oxford during the war, on colonial constitutions and especially his pioneering work *The Development of the Legislative Council*, his only substantial contribution to technical or professional history.[14] An assessment would have to be made of his impact as a teacher—as a young schoolmaster at Haileybury, as reader at the London School of Economics, as Professor of History and Dean of European Studies in the early, heroic period of the University of Sussex.

I want instead to focus your attention on one part of Martin Wight's legacy, *viz.* his ideas on the Theory of International Relations. First, I propose briefly to state what some of these ideas were. Secondly, I shall consider some questions that have long puzzled students of his work about the interpretation and assessment of these ideas. And thirdly I shall ask what can be learnt from Martin Wight's example.

When in the 1950s Wight was developing his lecture course at the London School of Economies the scientific or behaviourist movement towards what was called 'A Theory of International Relations' was gathering strength in the United States. This movement had its roots in dissatisfaction with what was taken to be the crude and obsolete methodology of existing general works about International Relations, especially those of Realist writers such as E.H. Carr, George F. Kennan and Hans Morgenthau, which formed the staple academic diet of the time. The hope that inspired the behaviourists was that by developing a more refined and up-to-date methodology it would be possible to arrive at a rigorously scientific body of knowledge that would help explain the past, predict the future and provide a firm basis for political action.

Wight's interest in the Theory of International Relations may also have owed something to dissatisfaction with the writings of the Realists, with which his own essay on *Power Politics* had close affinities, although his was a dissatisfaction with their substance rather than with their methodology. But the kind of theory to which he was drawn was utterly different from that which was intended by the behaviourists. He saw the Theory of International Relations—or, as he called it, International Theory—as a study in political philosophy or political speculation pursued by way of an examination of the main traditions of thought about International Relations in the past. Whereas the behaviourist school sought a kind of theory that approximated to science, his was a kind that approximated to philosophy. Whereas they began by rejecting the literature of the past, even the immediate past—and it was the latter they had in mind when they spoke, rather absurdly, of 'the traditionalists'—he began with the resolve to rediscover, to assemble and to categorise all that had been said and thought on the subject throughout the ages. While the behaviourists sought to exclude moral questions as lying beyond the scope of scientific treatment, Wight placed these questions at the centre of his inquiry. Where they hoped to arrive at 'A Theory of International Relations' that would put an end to disagreement and uncertainty Wight saw as the outcome of his studies simply an account of the debate among contending theories and doctrines, of which no resolution could be expected.

Wight's attitude towards the behaviourists was the source of one of my own disagreements with him. I felt that they represented a significant challenge and that it was important to understand them and engage in debate with them. The correct strategy, it appeared to me, was to sit at their feet, to study their position until one could state their own arguments better than they could and then—when they were least suspecting—to turn on them and slaughter them in an academic Massacre of Glencoe. Wight entertained none of these bloody thoughts. He made no serious effort to study the behaviourists and in effect ignored them. What this reflected, of course, was the much greater sense of confidence and security he had about his own position. The idea that an approach to Theory as unhistorical and unphilosophical as this might provide a serious basis for understanding world politics simply never entered his head.

At the heart of Martin Wight's Theory course was the debate between three groups of thinkers: the Machiavellians, the Grotians and the Kantians—or, as he sometimes called them (less happily, I think) the Realists, the Rationalists and the Revolutionists. The Machiavellians he thought of crudely as 'the blood and iron and immorality men', the Grotians as 'the law and order and keep your word men', and the Kantians as 'the subversion and liberation and missionary men'. Each pattern or tradition of thought embodied a description of the nature of international politics and also a set of prescriptions as to how men should conduct themselves in it.

For the Machiavellians—who included such figures as Hobbes, Hegel, Frederick the Great, Clémenceau, the twentieth century Realists such as Carr and Morgenthau—the true description of international politics was that it was international anarchy, a war of all against all or relationship of pure conflict among sovereign states. To the central question of the Theory of International Relations—'What is the nature of international society?'—the Machiavellians give the answer: there is no international society; what purports to be international society—the system of international law, the mechanism of diplomacy or today the United Nations—is fictitious. The prescriptions advanced by the Machiavellians were simply such as were advanced by Machiavelli in *The Prince*: it was for each state or ruler to pursue its own interest: the question of morality in international politics, at least in the sense of moral rules which restrained states in their relations with one another, did not arise.

For the Grotians—among whom Wight included the classical international lawyers, Locke, Burke, Castlereagh, Gladstone, Franklin Roosevelt, Churchill—international politics had to be described not as international anarchy but as international intercourse, a relationship chiefly among states to be sure, but one in which there was not only conflict but also cooperation. To the central question of Theory of International Relations the Grotians returned the answer that states, although not subject to a common superior, nevertheless formed a society—a society that was no fiction, and whose workings could be observed in institutions such as diplomacy, international law, the balance of power and the concert of great powers. States in their dealings with one another were not free of moral and legal restraints: the prescription of the Grotians was that states were bound by the rules of this international society they composed and in whose continuance they had a stake.

The Kantians rejected both the Machiavellian view that international politics was about conflict among states, and the view of the Grotians that it was about a mixture of conflict and cooperation among states. For the Kantians it was only at a superficial and transient level that international politics was about relations among states at all; at a deeper level it was about relations among the human beings of which states were composed. The ultimate reality was the community of mankind, which existed potentially, even if it did not exist actually, and was destined to sweep the system of states into limbo. The Kantians, like the Grotians, appealed to international morality, but what they understood by this was not the rules that required states to behave as good members of the society of states, but the revolutionary imperatives that required all men to work for human brotherhood. In the Kantian doctrine the world was divided between the elect, who were faithful to this vision of the community of mankind or *civitas maxima*, and the damned, the heretics, who stood in its way.

This Kantian pattern of thought, according to Wight, was embodied in the three successive waves of Revolutionist ideology that had divided modern international society on horizontal rather than vertical lines: that of the Protestant Reformation, that of the French Revolution and that of the Communist Revolution of our own times. But it was also embodied, he thought, in the Counter-Revolutionist ideologies to which each of these affirmations of horizontal solidarity gave rise: that of the Catholic Counter-Reformation, that of International Legitimism and that of Dullesian Anti-Communism.

Having identified these three patterns of thought Wight went on to trace the distinctive doctrines that each of them put forward concerning war, diplomacy, power, national interest, the obligation of treaties, the obligation of an individual to bear arms, the conduct of foreign policy and the relations between civilised states and so-called barbarians. It is impossible to summarise what Martin Wight had to say about the three traditions without in some measure vulgarising it. The impact of his lectures was produced not only by the grandeur of the design but also by the detailed historical embroidery, worked out with great subtlety, humanity and wit and with staggering erudition. In the hands of a lesser scholar the threefold categorisation would have served to simplify and distort the complexity of international thought. But Wight himself was the first to warn against the danger of reifying the concepts he had suggested. He insisted that the Machiavellian, Grotian and Kantian traditions were merely paradigms, to which no actual thinker did more than approximate: not even Machiavelli, for example, was in the strict sense a Machiavellian. Wight recognised that the exercise of classifying international theories requires that we have more pigeon-holes than three and so he suggested various ways in which each of the three traditions could be further subdivided: the Machiavellian tradition into its aggressive and its defensive form, the Grotian tradition into its realist and idealist form, the Kantian tradition into its evolutionary and its revolutionary forms, its imperialist and its cosmopolitanist forms, its historically backward-looking and its forward-looking or progressivist forms. He was always experimenting with new ways of formulating and describing the three traditions and in some versions of his lectures he suggested a fourth category of what he called Inverted Revolutionists, the pacifist stream of thought represented by the early Christians and by Tolstoy and Gandhi. He was aware that particular international thinkers in many cases straddle his categories: thus he explored, for example, the tension in Bismarck's thought between a Machiavellian perspective and a Grotian one, the tension in Woodrow Wilson between a Grotian perspective and a Kantian one, and the tension in Stalin between a Kantian perspective and a Machiavellian one. He saw the three traditions as forming a spectrum, within which at some points one pattern of thought merged with another, as infra-red becomes ultra-violet.

There are three questions about Wight's ideas on International Theory that I want to consider. First, as between the Machiavellian, the Grotian and the Kantian perspectives, where did Martin Wight himself stand? This was a question that earnest students would put to him plaintively at the end of a lecture. Wight used to delight in keeping students guessing on this issue and went out of his way to give them as little material as possible for speculating about it. In one of his lectures he quoted the following conversation of the earl of Shaftesbury: 'People differ in their discourse and profession about these matters, but men of sense are really but of one religion. ... "Pray, my lord, what religion is that which men of sense agree in?" "Madam," says the earl immediately, "men of sense never tell it."'[15]

Of course, if we had to put Martin Wight into one or another of his own three pigeon-holes there is no doubt that we should have to consider him a Grotian. Indeed, in one of the early versions of his lecture course he did actually say that he regarded the Grotians or Rationalists as 'the great central stream of European thought', and that he would regard it as the ideal to be a Grotian, while partaking of the realism of the Machiavellians, without their cynicism, and of the idealism of the Kantians, without their fanaticism. He displayed his leaning toward the Grotians when, in one of the chapters he wrote in *Diplomatic Investigations*, he gave an account of the Grotian tradition under the heading 'Western Values in International Relations', claiming that this tradition was especially representative of the values of Western civilisation because of its explicit connection with the political philosophy of constitutional government, and also because of its quality as a *via media* between extremes.[16] He was attracted towards the Grotian pattern of thought, I think, because he saw it as more faithful than either of the others to the complexity of international politics. He saw the Grotian approach to international morality, for example, as founded upon the recognition that the moral problems of foreign policy are complex, as against the view of the Kantians that these problems are simple, and the view of the Machiavellians that they are non-existent. The Grotian tradition, he thought, was better able to accommodate complexity because it was itself a compromise that made concessions to both the Machiavellian and the Kantian points of view. The Grotian idea of the just war, for example, was a compromise between the Kantian idea of the holy war or crusade and the Machiavellian idea of war as the *ultima ratio regum*. The Grotian idea that power in international society should be balanced and contained was a compromise between the Kantian demand that it should be abolished and the view of the Machiavellians that it was the object of the struggle. The view of the Grotians that the relations of the advanced countries with so-called barbarians should be based on the principle of trusteeship was a compromise between the Kantian notion that they should be based on liberation and assimilation, and the Machiavellian contention that they should be based on exploitation.

Nevertheless, it would be wrong to force Martin Wight into the Grotian pigeon-hole. It is a truer view of him to regard him as standing outside the three traditions, feeling the attraction of each of them but unable to come to rest within any one of them, and embodying in his own life and thought the tension among them. I have mentioned that as a young man Wight took up the position of an Inverted Revolutionist or pacifist. *Power Politics*, which he published at the age of thirty-three, is generally thought to embody a Machiavellian or Realist point of view and can certainly be linked more readily to the Machiavellian tradition than to the Grotian. As he grew older, it appears to me, the Grotian elements in his thinking became stronger: they are much more prominent in his contributions to *Diplomatic Investigations*, published in 1967, than in his earlier writings and reach their highest point in the essays on states systems which he wrote in the last years of his life. As one of the factors causing him to move closer to the Grotian perspective after he came to the London School of Economics, I should not myself discount the influence upon him of Professor Manning, despite the great contrasts in their respective approaches to the subject. I should not myself dare to speculate as to whether or not Professor Manning would classify himself as a Grotian. But certainly in his thinking the idea of international society occupies a central place and it emerges, I think, from the volume of essays presented to Professor Manning, to which Martin Wight contributed along with others among Manning's former colleagues and students, that there are certain common elements in the outlook of all those who worked in the Department at that time, no less noticeable in Wight's contribution than in the others.[17]

But Wight was too well aware of the vulnerability of the Grotian position ever to commit himself to it fully. He understood that it is the perspective of the international establishment. The speeches of Gladstone in the last century and of Franklin Roosevelt in this century proclaimed that their respective countries should seek in their foreign policies to conform to the common moral standards and sense of common interest of international society as a whole and in so doing they provided us with some of the most memorable statements of the Grotian idea. But what Wight asks us to notice about these two statesmen is that each of them, at the time he spoke, was the leader of the most powerful country in the world. The comfortable Grotian phrases do not come so readily to the lips of the oppressed, the desperate or the dissatisfied. In his lectures, as in his contribution to *The World in March 1939*, Wight expounds with remarkable detachment the critique put forward of Anglo–French Grotian legalism by Hitler in *Mein Kampf*: that Britain and France, the sated imperial powers, were like successful burglars now trying to settle down as country gentlemen, making intermittent appearances on the magistrate's bench.[18] Wight asks us to reflect on the fundamental truth lying behind Hitler's tedious phrases: that Britain and France had got where they were by struggle, that they could not contract out of the struggle at a moment that happened to suit them, still less could they justify themselves in attempting to contract out of it by appealing to moral principles which they had ignored when they were committed to the struggle.

If Wight could recognise the force of the Machiavellian critique of Grotian doctrines he is at first sight less capable of regarding sympathetically the Kantian critique of them. There was much about the Kantians—'The Political Missionaries or Fanatics', as he called them in early drafts of his lectures—that repelled him. He notes how the Kantians begin by repudiating all intellectual authorities, and any methodology save the principles of pure thought, but then become enslaved to sacred books; the Jacobins to Rousseau, the Communists to Marx. He saw it as the central paradox of the successive waves of revolutionist and counter-revolutionist doctrine that they aim at uniting and integrating the family of nations but in practice divide it more deeply than it was divided before. He held that these internal schisms of Western international society reflected the importation of attitudes which had previously prevailed in the external schism of Western international society and Islam. Just as in the Peloponnesian War the conflict between democratic and oligarchical factions imported into relations among Greeks the attitudes that previously had characterised the struggle between Hellenism and Medism, so in modern international history the various horizontal conflicts we have witnessed between the faithful and the heretical reproduce and reflect the earlier struggle between the Christian and the Infidel. The view that the Turk is Antichrist gives place to the view that the Pope—or some secular equivalent of him—is Antichrist; the epitaph of this historical connection between the internal and the external schisms of international society being the strange doctrine of Luther that Antichrist is the Pope and the Turk combined: the Pope his spirit and soul and the Turk his flesh and body.

Wight's in some respects negative attitude towards the Kantian tradition reflected his religious views. He saw the revolutionist and counter-revolutionist doctrines of modern times as perversions of the New Testament, secularised debasements of the story of the Messiah—just as he saw Hitler's National Socialism as a perversion of the Old Testament, the self-appointment of a new Chosen People. Wight was also repelled by progressivist doctrines of International Relations, which are found principally, although not I think exclusively, within the Kantian tradition and above all in Kant himself. One of Wight's most persistent themes is that in international politics by contrast with domestic politics progress has not taken place in modern times; that international politics is incompatible with progressivist theory; that in progressivist theories the conviction precedes the evidence; that 'it is not a good argument for a theory of international politics that we shall be driven to despair if we do not accept it'.

Wight's rejection of the belief in progress reflects, once again, not only his study of the evidence but his religious views. For him secular pessimism was the counterpart of theological optimism. 'Hope', as he once wrote, 'is not a political virtue; it is a theological virtue'.[19] Wight's lack of hope about the future of the secular world was, I think, so total, so crushing that only a deeply religious person could have sustained it. This lack of hope is most dramatically expressed in his invocation of de Maistre's 'occult and terrible law of the violent destruction of the human species'.[20] It is expressed also in his thesis that war is inevitable, even though particular wars are avoidable: a view he had the fortitude to contemplate because he was able to persuade himself that at the theological level this did not matter.[21] "For what matters," he said in a broadcast in 1948, "is not whether there is going to *be* another war or not, but that it should be recognised, if it comes, as an act of God's *Justice*, and if it is averted, as an act of God's *Mercy*."[22]

Yet there are moments when Wight seems as much drawn towards the Kantian tradition as towards the Machiavellian or the Grotian. He argues, in a long discussion of Kant's *Perpetual Peace*, that the progressivist argument from despair, while not intellectually speaking a 'good' argument, is nevertheless not a contemptible or dishonourable one: the optimism of a man who, like Kant, has looked into the abyss, but who says, 'No, looking down makes me giddy: I can only go on climbing if I look upward'—such an optimism grounded in utter despair merits respect. Wight also sees that the belief in progress is not the deepest element in the Kantian tradition. The deepest element—the element that must draw us to it—is the moral passion to abolish suffering and sin: the moral passion of Kant's hymn to duty, of Ivan Karamazov's cry that eternal harmony is not worth the tears of one tortured child, of Lenin's burning faith that suffering is not an essential part of life. Wight traces with care the distinction between the evolutionary Kantians, who believe that suffering is the cause of sin, and that if suffering can be abolished, sin can be abolished—and the revolutionary Kantians, such as Marx and Lenin, who believe that sin is the cause of suffering, and that suffering can be eradicated only if sin is first eradicated.

While Wight in his maturity was personally more drawn to the Grotian tradition than to either the Machiavellian or the Kantian, the essence of his teaching was that the truth about international politics had to be sought not in any one of these patterns of thought but in the debate among them. The three elements in international politics which they emphasised—the element of international anarchy stressed by the Machiavellians, the element of international intercourse, stressed by the Grotians and the element of the community of mankind, stressed by the Kantians—are all present. Wight's argument was that any attempt to describe the subject in terms of one of the cardinal elements to the exclusion of the others, was bound to break down.

There is a second question about what Martin Wight had to say that I wish to consider. Is it true? Can one really categorise the history of thought about international politics in this way? And if one can, does an account of the debate among the three traditions really advance our understanding of international politics in the twentieth century?

I believe myself that Wight tried to make too much of the debate among the three traditions Much that has been said about International Relations in the past cannot be related significantly to these traditions at all. Wight was, I believe, too ambitious in attributing to the Machiavellians, the Grotians and the Kantians distinctive views not only about war, peace, diplomacy, intervention and other matters of International Relations but about human psychology, about irony and tragedy, about methodology and epistemology. There is a point at which the debate Wight is describing ceases to be one that has actually taken place, and becomes one that he has invented; at this point his work is not an exercise in the history of ideas, so much as the exposition of an imaginary philosophical conversation, in the manner of Plato's dialogues.

I have already mentioned that Wight insisted that the three traditions were only to be taken as paradigms and that he was always urging us not to take what he said about them too seriously. But one has to take it seriously, or not at all. In all of Wight's work there is an instinct for the dramatic, a searching after superlatives—the *classic* expression of a point of view, the *earliest* statement of it, its *noblest* epitaph—that is the source of tantalising hypotheses and is what made his teaching so exciting. But one has to keep reminding oneself that the truth might be less dramatic, the superlatives not applicable, the hypotheses not fully tested. Again, in all his work there is an instinctive assumption—the legacy of Toynbee's impact upon him as a young man—that there is some rhythm or pattern in the history of ideas which is there, waiting to be uncovered. But we have to recognise the possibility that in some cases the rhythm or pattern may not be there at all. The defence he was inclined to put up—that he is merely putting forward suggestive paradigms or ideal types—will not do. It makes his position impregnable, but only at the price of making it equivocal.

But if the account of the three traditions will not bear all the weight that Martin Wight sought to place upon it, there is no doubt that it has a firm basis in reality. Anyone who seeks to write the history of thought about International Relations that Martin Wight himself was so superbly equipped to undertake will find it essential to build on the foundations which he laid. His analysis of the three traditions, moreover, was profoundly original. There is one passage in Gierke's account of the natural law tradition in which the germ of the idea is stated, but I have seen no evidence that Wight was aware of this passage and in any case it does not entail the great structure of ideas which, when fully grown in his mind, it became.[23]

That his account of these past traditions of thought contributes directly to our understanding of contemporary international politics there can be no doubt. In form his course was an exercise in the history of ideas, but in substance it was a statement about the world, including the world today. It presented the issues of contemporary international politics in historical and philosophical depth—requiring us, when confronted with some description of present events or some attitude taken up towards them, to view it as part of a series of recurrent descriptions or attitudes of the same kind, to identify the premises that lay behind it and to seek out the best of the arguments that had been presented, down the ages, for it and against it.

Wight's approach, it appears to me, provides an antidote to the narrow and introverted character of the professional academic debate about International Relations, the in-breeding and self-absorption of the journals and the textbooks, opening it out to wider intellectual horizons. It is striking that several of the current fashions within that professional debate have as their point of departure the discovery of some aspect of the subject which his own exposition of it has always embraced. The idea, for example, that international politics is not just a matter of relations between states, but also a matter of so-called 'transnational' relations among the individuals and groups that states compose, is one to which Martin Wight's exposition affords a central place; it is the core of the Kantian tradition. The notion which is central to the studies of models of future world order, now rising to a flood in Princeton and elsewhere, that it is necessary to look beyond the framework of the system of sovereign states and to contemplate alternative forms of universal political organisation—is one with which Wight was always concerned; one has only to think of his protest against 'the intellectual prejudice imposed by the sovereign state', his doctrine (derived from Toynbee) that the idea of the normalcy of the system of states is an optical illusion, and his attempt—in the essays on states systems—to explore the geographical and chronological boundaries of the modern states system, and to suggest some of the issues with which a general historical account of the main forms of universal political organisation—today, virtually uncharted territory—would have to be concerned. The recent revival of interest, in the Western world, in Marxist or Marxist–Leninist accounts of world politics, and the important neo-Marxist analyses of imperialism and neo-colonialism, fall into place quite naturally in Wight's presentation of the subject—even though it is true that he was not much interested in the economic dimension of the subject, and that his failure to deal with the history of thought about economic aspects of International Relations is one of the points at which he is vulnerable to criticism. Above all, perhaps, the rediscovery of moral questions by the political science profession, the realisation that International Relations is about ends as well as means—which is the only meaning we can give to what is now so portentously called 'the post-behavioural revolution'—merely takes us back to the point at which Wight began his inquiry.

Wight's approach also provided an antidote to the self-importance and self-pity that underlie the belief of each generation that its own problems are unique. 'One of the main purposes of university education', he wrote in his lecture notes, 'is to escape from the *Zeitgeist*, from the mean, narrow, provincial spirit which is constantly assuring us that we are the summit of human achievement, that we stand on the edge of unprecedented prosperity or unparalleled catastrophe, that the next summit conference is going to be the most fateful in history. ... It is a liberation of the spirit to acquire perspective, to recognise that every generation is confronted by problems of the utmost subjective urgency, but that an objective grading is probably impossible; to learn that the same moral predicaments and the same ideas have been explored before'.

Is there not a danger in following these injunctions that when confronted by some genuinely unprecedented situation we may fail to recognise it? Does not world politics in the twentieth century reflect developments—too obvious to enumerate—which it is correct to regard as without precedent, and is it not a delusion to imagine that these developments can be understood by the seeking out of historical parallels rather than by immersing ourselves in the study of what is recent and new, in all its individuality?

There is such a danger as this but it is not inherent in Wight's position. He did not maintain that every international political situation has an exact historical precedent or that fundamental change does not occur. Indeed, the conception of history as a storehouse of precedents that can be discovered and then applied as practical maxims of statecraft to contemporary political issues is one which he strongly attacked. He regarded this approach to history as the methodological gimmick of the Machiavellians—prominent in the writings of Carr and Morgenthau, as it had been earlier in those of the Social Darwinists, traceable back to the view of Bolingbroke that 'history is philosophy teaching by examples', and resting ultimately on Machiavelli's own assumption that laws of politics could be derived from history because history took the form of mechanically recurring cycles.

There is a third question I want to consider. In what sense did Martin Wight think that theoretical inquiry in International Relations is possible? Wight's most famous article on International Theory bears the title 'Why Is There No International Theory?'[24] This leads students to ask: does he believe in International Theory or does he not? How can he deny the existence of the enterprise he is engaged in? Brian Porter has recently suggested that there is no great puzzle about this: what Wight meant was that the student will not find the history of thought about International Relations in ready-made and accessible form: the pieces of the jigsaw puzzle have to be disinterred and put together.[25] This is the correct explanation of the title, and it is confirmed by the fact that in an early draft Wight used as his heading 'Why Is There no *Body* of International Theory?'

But there is a deeper problem in this article than the one posed by its title. Wight argues that it is no accident that International Relations has never been the subject of any great theoretical work, that there is 'a kind of disharmony between international theory and diplomatic practice, a kind of recalcitrance of international politics to being theorised about'.[26] He notes that the only acknowledged classic of International Relations—Thucydides on the *Peloponnesian War*—is a work not of theory but of history. And he goes on to say that 'the quality of international politics, the preoccupations of diplomacy, are embodied and communicated less in works of political and international theory than in historical writings'.[27]

Is Wight here proclaiming the ultimate heresy that after all, theoretical understanding of international politics is not possible, only historical understanding? Is he, so to speak, throwing in the sponge? No, he is not; this is not what he says and all of his work in this field is a denial of it—for while that work is steeped in history it is not itself history. Wight gives us the clue a little further on when he writes that the only kind of theoretical inquiry that is possible is 'the kind of rumination about human destiny to which we give the unsatisfactory name philosophy of history'.[28]

Theoretical inquiry into International Relations is therefore philosophical in character. It does not lead to cumulative knowledge after the manner of natural science. Confronted by a controversy, like the great debate which Wight explores among the three traditions, we may identify the assumptions that are made in each camp, probe them, juxtapose them, relate them to circumstances, but we cannot expect to settle the controversy except provisionally, on the basis of assumptions of our own that are themselves open to debate. All of this must follow once we grant Wight's initial assumption that theoretical inquiry into International Relations is necessarily about moral or prescriptive questions.

I believe myself, however, that an inquiry that is philosophical can be more public, more rational, more disciplined than Wight was willing to allow. In his work we may note a preference for vagueness over precision, for poetic imagery over prosaic statement, for subjective judgement over explicit formulation of a line of argument. I do not think, for example, that 'rumination' is an adequate word to describe the activity of theoretical analysis. Wight speaks of the 'fruitful imprecision' of Grotius's language, but it appears to me that this imprecision is in no way fruitful.[29] It is true, as Wight says, that the stuff of international theory is constantly bursting the bounds of the language in which we try to handle it, but this appears to me a reason for trying to find a language that is appropriate. There is a tendency to believe that those who are profound, as Martin Wight undoubtedly was, are thereby licensed to be obscure. This is the point at which I begin to part company with Martin Wight and to wonder whether there was not, after all, some value in the demand of the behaviourists that International Theory be put on a proper methodological footing.

I have tried in this lecture not to lose sight of those aspects of Wight's work with which it is possible to quarrel. Let me mention some more of them. The term Wight used to describe the enterprise he was engaged in—International Theory—is not a good one; as Professor Manning pointed out long ago it is the Relations that are International not the Theory; the enterprise is better described as Theory of International Relations.

Wight's contribution is vulnerable to the charge of being unduly Eurocentric. It is the glory of his work that it sprang from a mastery of Western culture, ancient and medieval no less than modern. But although he took some account of Islam and of Gandhi and played with the idea that there was a Chinese equivalent of the debate among the three traditions—in the conflict of Confucianism, Taoism and the School of Law—he had no deep understanding of non-Western civilisations. He saw modern international society as the product of Western culture and felt, I think, a basic doubt as to how far the non-Western majority of states today have really been incorporated within it. I should not myself leap to the conclusion that in this he was wrong, but he does sometimes display insensitivity about non-Western peoples and their aspirations today, as in his contemptuous dismissal of Kautilya or his comparison between the Afro–Asian powers and the revisionist powers of the 1930s.

Wright's immense learning sometimes does more to encumber than to enrich his arguments: his intellectual architecture is not so much classical as baroque. His learning is entirely authentic: Wight was not a cultural showman or pedant, and had a great gift of apt quotation. But in some of his writings the branches of the tree are so weighed down with historical foliage that it is difficult to find the trunk.

I have often felt uneasy about the extent to which Wight's view of International Relations derives from his religious beliefs. These beliefs are not obtrusive in his writings about secular matters, which apparently employ only the ordinary canons of empirical knowledge of the world. And yet one is conscious of the extent to which his view of the subject is affected by beliefs not derived in this way.

What can one learn from Martin Wight's example? He was a person of unique gifts and no one else is likely to contribute to the subject in quite the way that he did. But three aspects of his work in this field are worthy of note by others.

The first is his view that theoretical inquiry into International Relations should be focused upon the moral and normative presuppositions that underlie it. In the 1950s and 1960s there was a tendency in the Western world to leave these presuppositions out of account: to inquire into the international system without inquiring into its moral and cultural basis, to discuss policy choices—as in strategic studies or development economics—in terms of means or techniques rather than in terms of ends. More recently, values or ends have made a comeback, but chiefly in the form of the shouting of slogans, the fashion of so-called political commitment, which means that values are asserted and at the same time held to be beyond examination. Wight stood, it appears to me, not simply for having value premises but for inquiring into them.

The second is his attempt to associate theoretical inquiry with historical inquiry. The professional diplomatic historians, on the whole, have not been interested in large questions of theory. The theorists of International Relations have lacked the capacity or the inclination to do the historical work. Or they have approached it in the belief that it consists of "data", to be fed into the computer, and without any real grasp of historical inquiry itself. Wight is one of the few to have bridged this gap with distinction.

The third and the most important is Wight's very deep commitment to intellectual values and to the highest academic standards. Especially, perhaps, in a field such as International Relations there is a temptation to study what is ephemeral rather than of enduring importance, to be knowing rather than to say only what one truly knows, to claim results prematurely rather than to persist in the long haul. The most impressive thing about Martin Wight was his intellectual and moral integrity and *gravitas*. His writings are marked by paucity, but at least we cannot say of them, as he said of theoretical writings about

International Relations before him, that they are marked also by intellectual and moral poverty.

(3) The Revolt against the West

By the time of the First World War, there existed not only a worldwide international system but also an international society that was universal in the sense that it covered all the world and included states from Asia, Africa, and the Americas as well as Europe. In this universal international society, however, a position of dominance was still occupied by the European powers, or more broadly (since Europe's offshoots in north and south America, southern Africa, and Australasia partook of this dominance) by the Western powers, which continued to occupy this position until the Second World War. After the Second World War a revolt against Western dominance—a revolt which had been growing in strength earlier in the century, and whose roots lay late in the last century—became powerful enough to shake the system.

The dominance of the European or Western powers at the turn of the century was expressed not only in their superior economic and military power and in their commanding intellectual and cultural authority but also in the rules and institutions of international society. This society was still seen as an association of mainly European and Christian states, to which outside political communities could be admitted only if and when they met the criteria for membership laid down by the founding members—as Japan by 1900 was widely deemed to have done and China not yet to have done. The rules of international law which then prevailed had been made, for the most part, by these European or Western states, which had consented to them through custom or treaties concluded among themselves; the governments and peoples of Asia, Africa, and Oceania, who were subject to these rules, had not given their consent to them. The international legal rules, moreover, were not only made by the European or Western powers, they were also in substantial measure made *for* them: part, at least, of the content of the then existing international law (e.g. treaty law, which upheld the validity of treaties concluded under duress; the law of state sovereignty, which took no account of the self-determination of peoples; the law governing the use of force, which made resort to force a prerogative right of states) served to facilitate the maintenance of European or Western ascendancy.

At the turn of the century the chief pillars of this system of dominance were the European colonial powers, especially Britain and France, and to a lesser extent the latecomers, Germany and Italy; and even as late as the early years of the Second World War, this still appeared to be the case. But the United States, the white dominions of the British Empire, the Latin American republics, and indeed the Russian Empire were also supporters and beneficiaries of Western dominance, even if in some cases ambiguously; and as the revolt unfolded against it, later in the century, they too became its targets.

The United States, it is true, saw itself as an anti-colonial power, sympathised with anti-colonial rhetoric, which was the rhetoric of its own war of independence, and resented the exclusiveness of European imperial structures, in which its trade was sometimes put at a disadvantage. But the American colonies which gained their independence from Britain were themselves a product of the process of European expansion; the United States carried this process further by extending its dominion across the north American continent to consolidate its territory, subjugating aboriginal peoples as it did so; it expanded in the Caribbean and the Pacific to become a colonial power in its own right; its denial of equal rights to black Americans aligned it with European policies of racial exclusiveness; and the economic position it acquired for itself in Asia and Africa was such that, when European colonial rule eventually disappeared and neo-colonialism became the principal target of Third World protest, the United States came to be viewed as the main antagonist.

Russia, it is true, has always been perceived in Europe as semi-Asiatic in character, a perception confirmed by the ambivalence in Russia's own mind as to whether it belongs to the West or not; it was, until recently, a relatively backward and under-developed country, vulnerable to the Western great powers as Asian countries have been; the efforts of Russian reformers, from Peter the Great onwards, to learn from the West so as to be able to compete with it provide a model which Asians and Africans have followed; and since 1917 the Soviet state has rendered powerful assistance to the forces struggling against Western dominance as their ally and champion. But like the United States, the imperial Russia of the turn of the century was the product of European expansion; like the maritime expansion of the Western European states, the expansion of Russia by land proceeded by the subjugation of indigenous communities and immigration and settlement by metropolitan peoples. Its frontiers, determined in places by 'unequal treaties', and its non-European peoples, originally subject to Russian dominance, still partly define the character of the Soviet Union today, rendering it also a potential target of Third World hostility.

The Latin American republics, like the United States, have an anti-colonial and national liberationist tradition. In the late nineteenth and early twentieth centuries, moreover, at a time when the United States saw itself as a newly arrived great power, the Latin American states saw themselves as victims of great power dominance and intervention; their attempts to impose legal limitations on the use of force in international relations and to strengthen the principle of non-intervention were an anticipation of the later policies of the Third World. In the post-colonial world their posture in world affairs has been that of poor, under-developed states, allied with Asians and Africans in the Group of 77 and the Non-Aligned Movement. But they, too, are the products of the process of European expansion; they are founded upon the subjugation of aboriginal peoples, whom some of them continue to oppress; they are chiefly

Western in language, religion, and other aspects of culture, and if anything distinguishes their position from that of the United States in the context of the revolt against Western dominance, it is only their conspicuous failure to match it in economic or political development.

European or Western dominance of the universal international society may be said to have reached its apogee about the year 1900. It is true that at that time the Western impact on the world was in many respects less far-reaching than it has since become. European colonial expansion did not reach to its fullest extent until the period between the two world wars. African and Asian societies, even under colonial rule, were not then as entangled in the world economy as they were to become in the post-colonial period. The technological distances between the most advanced Western societies and most Asian and African societies, although this is difficult to measure, may be judged to be in some respects greater now than it was then. The intellectual and cultural penetration of Asian and African societies by the West was less profound then than it was to become later.

But at the turn of the century the dominance of the European or Western powers expressed a sense of self-assurance, both about the durability of their position in international society and about its moral purpose, that did not survive the First World War. In non-Western societies also the ascendancy of the West was still widely regarded as a fact of nature rather than as something which could or should be changed. The spiritual or psychological supremacy of the West was at its highest point, even if its material or technological supremacy was not. In their attitudes to other peoples, moreover, the Western powers displayed a measure of unity, of which a striking expression in 1900 was their intervention in China to suppress the Boxer Rising. The leading states of the old, European-dominated international order sank their differences and sent an international army that inflicted humiliation upon the greatest of non-Western societies. The presence in this international army of a Japanese contingent, however, showed that the system was already changing. The Japanese did not respond to the Dowager Empress's request to the Mikado for Asian unity against the West, but joined in the defence of the international society of states, to membership of which they had graduated.

The revolt against Western dominance, which had already begun at this time, comprised five phases or themes. First, there was what we may call the struggle for equal sovereignty. This was the struggle of those states which retained their formal independence, but enjoyed only a subordinate or inferior status, to achieve equal rights as sovereign states. The marks of their inferiority included so-called 'unequal treaties'—treaties concluded under duress, conferring conspicuously unequal benefits on the parties to them, and impairing the sovereignty of the non-Western states concerned—and especially those conferring rights of extraterritorial jurisdiction on the citizens of Western states within the territories of non-Western states. The lead in this struggle was taken by Japan, which freed itself of extraterritorial jurisdiction in the course of the 1890s, and went on to achieve the status not merely of a sovereign state equal in rights to the Western powers, but of a great power able to impose 'unequal treaties' of its own on Korea and China. Turkey achieved the elimination of extraterritorial jurisdiction through the Treaty of Lausanne in 1923 (the system had been unilaterally repudiated by the Ottoman Empire on entering the war in 1914, but re-imposed by the victorious Allies through the Treaty of Sèvres in 1920); Egypt through the Anglo–Egyptian Treaty of 1936; China through agreement with the United States and Britain in 1943. In the Persian Gulf, where the old international order survived for a period after it had disappeared elsewhere, as the Empire of Trebizond survived the fall of Byzantium, extraterritorial jurisdiction continued until the British withdrawal in 1971.

Secondly, there was the anti-colonial revolution, by which we normally mean the struggle of Asian, African, Caribbean, and Pacific peoples for formal political independence of European and American colonial rule, although it is worth noting that Korea between 1912 and 1945 was a colony not of any European power but of Japan, that the Sudan between 1899 and 1956 was a quasi-colony of Egypt in conjunction with Britain, and that the European peoples of Cyprus and Malta still had the status of colonial dependencies after the Second World War. Although the colonial system was disturbed by the prominence given to the principle of national self-determination in the Bolshevik Revolution, the 1919 Peace Settlement, and the evolution of the British Commonwealth in the interwar period, the revolution that overthrew it in the non-Western world belongs chiefly to the post-1945 era: the Asian colonial dependencies became independent for the most part in the late 1940s and 1950s, the African territories in the 1960s and 1970s. With the collapse of the Portuguese empire in 1974–75 the era of classic, European colonialism came to an end, even though the anti-colonial movement had further targets in white minority rule in southern Africa and Jewish rule in Palestine.

Thirdly, there has been the struggle for racial equality, or more accurately the struggle of non-white states and peoples against white supremacism. The old Western-dominated international order was associated with the privileged position of the white race: the international society of states was at first exclusively, and even in its last days principally, one of white states; non-white peoples everywhere, whether as minority communities within these white states, as majority communities ruled by minorities of whites, or as independent peoples dominated by white powers, suffered the stigma of inferior status. The struggle to change this state of affairs spans many centuries and touches the internal history of states as well as their relations with one another. It encompasses the eighteenth-century doctrine of the rights of man, at first applied effectively only to persons of European race, the movements for abolition of slavery and the slave trade in Europe and America, the emergence of Haiti as a black state, the Japanese victories over Russia in 1904–1905 and the Western powers in 1941–42, the pan-African movement in the first half of the century. But it has been in the post-1945 period that the decisive changes have come: the Afro-Asian movement launched at Bandung in 1955; the achievement of independence by so many non-white states that the whites have become a minority; the victories of the civil rights movement in the United States in the 1950s and 1960s, profound in its repercussions on other Western countries; the virtual expulsion of South Africa from the Commonwealth, and its reduction to the status of a pariah in the United Nations; the development of human rights instrumentalities under the aegis of the United Nations, and especially the Convention on Elimination of Racial Discrimination of 1966. The solidarity of non-whites against whites has been one of the principal elements making for the cohesion of the loose coalition of states and movements to which we refer as the Third World.

Fourthly, there has been the struggle for economic justice. Although anti-colonial movements from the beginning maintained that imperialism was bound up with economic exploitation, and included goals of economic development or betterment in their programs, and although the assertion by Third World states of sovereignty over their natural resources may be traced back through the nationalisation of the Anglo-Iranian oil company in 1951, the Mexican expropriations of foreign oil in companies of the 1930s, the experience of the Bolshevik Revolution, and in the Calvo and Drago doctrines asserted by Latin American states late in the last century against foreign intervention in their economic affairs, it was not until the 1960s that economic objectives attained pride of place in the agenda of the coalition of Asian, African, and Latin American states, which by then had become known as the Third World. By the time of the formation of the Group of 77 at the first meeting in 1964 of the UN Conference on Trade, Aid, and Development, concern about colonialism was giving place to concern about economic domination by the Western powers of the post-colonial world; the gap between the living standards of most Western and most Third World states was growing as a consequence not only of the economic boom in Western countries but also of their new policies of state promotion of minimum standards of welfare; and consciousness of the gap was growing as a result of the revolution in communications. In the 1960s the debate between Western and Third World countries over what was called international development assistance took the form of a discussion of the terms of a partnership between rich and poor countries that had common interests in development—the rich having a stake in the development of the poor, and the poor in the further development of the rich. In the 1970s by contrast, under the impact of the 1973–74 oil crisis, the world recession, the radicalisation of Third World opinion and the reaction against this in the West, the terms of the debate changed: the idea of a partnership between rich and poor gave place to that of a struggle for

119

the world product, non-zero sum conceptions of the relationship to zero-sum, development assistance to redistribution of wealth—a change reflected in 1974 in the Declaration of a New International Economic Order and the Charter of the Economic Rights and Duties of States endorsed by Third World majorities in the United Nations.

Fifthly, there has been the struggle for what is called cultural liberation: the struggle of non-Western peoples to throw off the intellectual or cultural ascendancy of the Western world so as to assert their own identity and autonomy in matters of the spirit. The revolt against Western dominance in relation to the four earlier themes that have been mentioned has been conducted, as least ostensibly, in the name of ideas or values that are themselves Western, even if it is not clear in all cases that these ideas are exclusively or uniquely Western: the rights of states to sovereign equality, the rights of nations to self-determination, the rights of human beings to equal treatment irrespective of race, their rights to minimum standards of economic and social welfare. Perhaps the right to cultural autonomy may also be regarded as a Western value, or at all events as a value which Western countries (for example, as signatories of the Covenant on Economic, Social and Cultural Rights of 1966) now support. But the re-assertion by Asian, African, and other non-Western peoples of their traditional and indigenous cultures, as exemplified in Islamic fundamentalism, Hindu and Sikh traditionalism in India, manifestations of ethnic consciousness in Africa, has raised the question whether what has been widely interpreted as a revolt against Western dominance carried out in the name of Western values, is not a revolt against Western values as such.

We need to bear in mind, in speaking of the repudiation of 'Western values' in Third World countries, that the former are neither monolithic nor unchanging. Different Western countries, and different regimes within those countries, stand and have stood for values of very different kinds: in the post-1945 period the West for some Third World peoples has been represented by the resurgent imperialism of the French Fourth Republic and the post-war Netherlands, by the Spanish and Portuguese dictatorships, and by a South African government committed to strengthening rather than removing barriers between races. In the period during which the revolt against Western dominance has been unfolding, there have been vast changes in the values prevailing in all Western societies; public attitudes towards the equal rights of non-Western states, national liberation from colonial rule, equal rights of non-white races, the rights of poor peoples to economic justice and cultural autonomy have been transformed in recent decades. Moreover, in noting the gap between Third World behaviour and what Western persons like to think of as 'Western values', we should not fall into the error of assuming that Western peoples are themselves always faithful to them; they are at most a statement of Western ideals, not a description of Western practices.

Yet as Asian, African, and other non-Western peoples have assumed a more prominent place in international society it has become clear that in matters of values the distance between them and Western societies is greater than, in the early years of national liberation or decolonisation, it was assumed to be. In making their demands for equal rights on behalf of oppressed states, nations, races, or cultures, the leaders of the Third World spoke as suppliants, in a world in which the Western powers were still in a dominant position. The demands that they made had necessarily to be put forward in terms of charters of rights (the Declaration of the Rights of Man and the Citizen, the American Declaration of Independence, the League Covenant, the Atlantic Charter, the UN Charter) of which Western powers were the principal authors. The moral appeal had to be cast in the terms that would have most resonance within Western societies. But as Asian, African, and other non-Western peoples have become stronger relative to the Western powers, they have become freer to adopt a different rhetoric that sets Western values aside, or at all events places different interpretations upon them.

The collapse of the old, Western-dominated international order has been brought about by perhaps five factors on which we may briefly touch. First, there has been the psychological or spiritual awakening of Asian and African, Caribbean and Pacific peoples, beginning among small groups of the Western-educated, later affecting masses of people, that led them to perceive the old order no longer as a fact of nature, but as something that could be changed, to recognise that by mobilising themselves to this end they could indeed change it, to abandon a passive for a politically active role in world affairs. The great instrument these peoples have used to advance their purposes has been the state: they began by capturing control of states and then used them—domestically to build nationhood, to establish control of their economies, to combat local vestiges of external dominance; internationally to establish relations with outside states, to combine with their friends, drive wedges among their enemies, and expound their views in the councils of the world.

A second factor has been a weakening of the will on the part of the Western powers to maintain their position of dominance; or at least to accept the costs necessary to do so. The First World War destroyed the self-assurance of the European powers which had been so cardinal a feature of the old order, while also leading them to embrace a principle of national self-determination contradictory of the legitimacy of colonial rule. The Second World War left the European imperial powers too weak to maintain old kinds of dominance, even though it left the United States with a commanding position in world affairs. As Third World peoples mobilised themselves politically in defence of their interests, the use of force to maintain Western positions of dominance became more costly. At the same time it came to be questioned whether colonial dependencies were a source of material gain: the old liberal thesis, that the true interests of the metropolitan peoples lay in non-interventionism and avoidance of empire, was revived, and appeared to be confirmed by the economic triumphs of Germany and Japan, achieved without military pre-eminence or colonies. Nor were the peoples of the metropolitan countries always insensitive to the aspirations of non-Western peoples: both in Europe and in America there were many for whom the emancipation of the former dependencies represented the fulfilment of their own ideals.

It would be wrong, however, to countenance the idea that the Western powers offered little or no resistance to the dismantling of the old order, or that this dismantling came about essentially in response to their own policies. That the process of de-colonisation was an act of policy of the colonial powers themselves is the thesis both of apologists for the policies of the colonial powers (as in the argument of writers about the British Commonwealth that the purpose of empire was preparation for self-government), and of those who see the transition from colonialism to neo-colonialism, from direct to indirect domination, as the result of a conspiracy by the colonial powers themselves to bring about a form of domination that they had come to prefer. There were indeed cases in the latter stages of the process of national liberation, especially in Africa and the Pacific, in which the independence of former colonies came about through cooperation between the metropolitan power and local representatives. But such instances were made possible only by the fact that the will of the colonial powers had already been broken. The reverses that were inflicted upon the Western powers in Indonesia, Indo-China, Algeria, Suez, Cyprus, Vietnam, and elsewhere had first to be suffered before the lessons from them could be drawn.

A third factor making for the demise of the old order was the impact of the Bolshevik revolution and the rise of the Soviet Union as a major power. The influence of the Soviet Union, it is true, has not always been perceived as a positive one from the point of view of the Afro-Asian or Third World nationalist struggles. Classical Marxism was basically unsympathetic to nationalism, and although Leninism has aligned the communist movement with it, the heritage of the ideas of Marx and Engels has sometimes proved a handicap in this respect. Stalin's Russia during the Second World War was aligned with European imperialists against Germany, and thus withdrew its support for anti-imperialist movements. Even after the War, Soviet support for communist revolution in the Third World stood in the way of an understanding with Third World nationalism until after the death of Stalin. The Soviet Union has never been able to compete with the United States and the Western European countries in providing economic and technological assistance to Third World countries. The Soviet Union's frontiers, as we noted above, result from European expansion and subjugation of non-European peoples, which means that some Third World sentiment may be mobilised against it, as China has sought to do. The Soviet Union's capacity for direct military intervention in Third World countries, demonstrated in Afghanistan since 1979, has attracted some of the Third World antagonism against external domination previously directed chiefly at the Western powers.

Nevertheless, the rise of Soviet power, especially since the Second World War, including its attainment of crude strategic parity with the United States by the early 1970s and development of global interventionary capacity, has been basically helpful to the struggle of Third World peoples against the dominance of the Western powers. It is not merely, or perhaps even chiefly, that the Soviet state has provided a model of socialist planning and control of economic, social, and political life that has exerted an immense attraction over Third World countries and movements. It is rather that, since the collapse of Germany and Japan, the Soviet Union has been the chief centre of power in world affairs outside Western Europe and North America. Since it is the established ascendancy of Western Europe and North America in Asia, Africa, and Latin America that the Third World has been struggling to overthrow, the alliance of the Third World and the Soviet Union against the West, at least on a limited range of issues, that has been a basic feature of world affairs for many decades, has been natural and perhaps inevitable.

A fourth factor assisting the efforts of non-Western states and peoples to transform the system has been the existence of a more general equilibrium of power, to which the rise of the Soviet Union contributed, but of which it was only part, that has operated to the benefit of those challenging the old order. It is not a new circumstance that 'divisions among the imperialists' should operate in favour of the independence of weak peoples. But from the very beginning of the process of Western expansion, when the Papacy sought to contain the rivalry between Spain and Portugal, there were attempts, often successful, to preserve a common front *vis-à-vis* the non-Christian or extra-European world, or at least a common framework for competition within it. We have noted how, in the nineteenth century, such a framework was provided by the Concert of Europe.

In the post-1945 world also some elements of this common framework still survive: it is not wholly fanciful, for example, to see in the tacit understandings through which the North Atlantic powers and the Soviet Union have excluded war from their own area of the world, while exporting their military conflicts to the periphery, an echo of the arrangements reached between France and Spain at the Peace of Cateau-Cambrésis in 1559, whereby armed conflicts in the New World were allowed to continue on the understanding that they would not disturb the peace of Europe. It is clear, however, that the divisions among the advanced powers are today much deeper than they were at the time when the West could agree to send an international force with a German commander to keep a dissident China in order; and that this new circumstance has operated to assist the weaker members of the system. Deeply divided as they are, the North

Atlantic states and the Soviet Union serve to check one another's interventions in the Third World. At the same time, the existence of several major centres of power—in Western Europe, Japan, and China, as well as in the United States and the Soviet Union—provides Third World countries with a range of diplomatic options for combining with one major power against another.

Finally, the dismantling of the old order has been assisted by a transformation of the legal and moral climate of international relations which the Third World states themselves, grouped with one another in the Afro-Asian movement, the Non-Aligned Movement, and the Group of 77, have played the principal role in bringing about. Commanding majorities of votes as they do in the political organs of the United Nations, and able to call upon the prestige of numbers, not merely of states but of persons, accruing to the states claiming to represent a majority of the world's population, they have overturned the old structure of international law and organisation that once served to sanctify their subject status. The equal rights of non-Western states to sovereignty, the rights of non-Western peoples to self-determination, the rights of non-white races to equal treatment, non-Western peoples to economic justice, and non-Western cultures to dignity and autonomy—these rights are today clearly spelt out in conventions having the force of law, even though in many cases they are not enjoyed in practice and no consensus exists about their meaning and interpretation.

The Western powers have fought a rearguard action against this rewriting of international law and quasi-law, which may be studied in the debates that led up to the passing of such historic resolutions of UN organs as the 1960 Declaration on the Granting of Independence to Colonial Peoples, the 1965 resolution recognising the right to use force in a war of national liberation, or the 1974 Declaration of a New International Economic Order. As a result of the challenge delivered by the Third World to the old legal order there is today deep division between the Western powers and Third World states about a wide range of normative issues. As the political organs of the United Nations were made to subserve the political purposes of the Third World coalition, the Western powers, once able to make the United Nations the instrument of purposes of their own, became disillusioned about it. It is possible to argue that as a consequence of these disagreements and attempts to paper them over by resort to concepts of 'soft law', the integrity of international law has been debased and the role actually played by international law in international relations, as opposed to what John Austin once called positive international morality, has gone into decline. It is not possible, however, to doubt that the changes wrought by Third World majorities have affected the legal and moral climate of world politics profoundly, and in such a way as to assist the challenge to Western dominance.

Theorists of international 'dependence' tell us that the position of the Western countries in the international system is still one of dominance. It is indeed true that the present distribution of wealth and power in the world falls far short of the aspirations of Third World peoples and their well-wishers elsewhere for justice and equality. But if we compare the position occupied by non-Western states and peoples in the universal international society of today with the position in which they found themselves at the turn of the century, it is difficult not to feel that the revolt against Western dominance has had a measure of success.

ENDNOTES

[1] Ali A. Mazrui, *Towards a Pax Africana: A Study of Ideology and Ambition*, Weidenfeld & Nicolson, London, 1966.

[2] Augustine, *The City of God*, Book XIX, C.XIII, Everyman edition, London, 1950, p. 249.

[3] See Quincy Wright, *The Role of International Law in the Elimination of War*, Manchester University Press, Manchester, p. 7.

[4] See Myres S. McDougal and Associates, *Studies in World Public Order*, Yale University Press, New Haven, CT, 1960.

[5] The distinctions between general and particular justice, formal and substantive, arithmetical and proportionate, commutative and distributive, are all to be found in Aristotle. For a contemporary analysis, see Morris Ginsberg, *On Justice in Society*, Cornell University Press, Ithaca, NY, 1965.

[6] Aristotle, *Laws*, Book VI, p. 757.

[7] Telford Taylor, *Nuremberg and Vietnam, an American Tragedy*, Quadrangle Books, Chicago, 1970.

[8] See Kenneth Boulding, 'The Concept of World Interest', in Bert F. Hoselitz (ed.), *Economics and the Idea of Mankind*, Columbia University Press, New York, 1965; C. Wilfred Jenks, *The Common Law of Mankind*, Frederick A. Praeger, Inc., New York, 1958; and Richard A. Falk, *This Endangered Planet: Prospects and Proposals for Human Survival*, Vintage Books, New York, 1972.

[9] Boulding, 'The Concept of World Interest', p. 55.

[10] Julius Stone, 'Approaches to the Notion of International Justice', in C. Black and Richard A. Falk (eds), *The Future of the international Legal Order, Volume.1: Trends and Patterns*, Princeton University Press, Princeton, NJ, 1969.

[11] Mazrui, *Towards a Pax Africana*, p. 137.

[12] Sir Herbert Butterfield, *Raison D'Etat. The Inaugural Martin Wight Memorial Lecture*, Sussex University, 1975.

[13] Martin Wight, *Power Politics*, Royal Institute of International Affairs, London, 1946.

[14] *The Development of the Legislative Council 1601–1946*, London, 1946.

[15] Earl of Shaftesbury quoted in *The New York Law Journal*, 18 November 1963, p. 4, column 4.

[16] See H. Butterfield and M. Wight (eds), *Diplomatic Investigations: Essays in the Theory of International Politics*, Allen and Unwin, London, 1966, pp. 89–131.

[17] See A.M. James (ed.), *The Bases of International Order: Essays in Honour of C.A.W. Manning*, Oxford University Press, London, 1973.

[18] See Arnold Toynbee and F.T. Ashton-Gwatkin (eds), *The World in March 1939: Survey of International Affairs 1939–1946*, Oxford University Press for the Royal Institute of International Affairs, London, 1952.

[19] 'Christian Commentary', talk on the B.B.C. Home Service, 29 October 1948.

[20] Butterfield and Wight (eds), *Diplomatic Investigations*, pp. 33–34.

[21] For Martin Wight's discussion of the inevitability of war, see 'War and International Politics', *The Listener*, 13 October 1953.

[22] See 'Christian Commentary', talk on the B.B.C. Home Service, 29 October 1948.

[23] See Otto von Gierke, *Natural Law and the Theory of Society 1500 to 1860* (trans. Ernest Barker), Beacon Press, Boston, p. 85.

24 Butterfield and Wight (eds), *Diplomatic Investigations*, ch. I.

25 See Brian Porter's unpublished paper, 'Martin Wight's "International Theory": Some Reflections'.

26 Butterfield and Wight (eds), *Diplomatic Investigations*, p. 33.

27 Butterfield and Wight (eds), *Diplomatic Investigations*, p. 32.

28 Butterfield and Wight (eds), *Diplomatic Investigations*, p. 33.

29 Butterfield and Wight (eds), *Diplomatic Investigations*, p. 102.

Chapter 9

Lost Friend

Michael Howard

When Alastair Buchan died, as tragically though more suddenly as did Hedley himself, Hedley was at the time in Oxford, as a Visiting Fellow at All Souls; and our first reaction on recovering from the shock of Alastair's death was to urge Hedley to apply for the Chair.[1] He was so very much the obvious candidate. Alastair with his driving energy, his flair for organisation and his global network of friendships, political as well as academic, had laid the foundations for a great school of international relations. What we now needed was an intellectual leader of outstanding calibre who could build on those foundations and give the school that distinction (in the literal sense of the word) which would enable it to make up for its late start and make Oxford as admirable and admired in this field as it was already in so many other.

There was to my mind literally no one better qualified to take on this task than Hedley. I had known him since his early days at the London School of Economics—where he had made his mark from the very beginning, in that richly talented team put together by Charles Manning—as a scintillatingly original mind. Alastair, with his genius for talent-spotting, singled him out act as draftsman and rapporteur for the ISS Conference here in Oxford 1960, which resulted in his first book *The Control of the Arms Race*. I can still vividly recall the sessions where veteran disarmers, bureaucrats and warriors shook their heads over the lucid draft chapters, clear, uncompromising, sensible, in which this tall, diffident yet abrasive young man cut through half a century's emotional waffle and forced them to think again from first principles. It was this experience which first cast Hedley in the role of the *enfant terrible* of International Relations; one whose impatience with political cant and academic folly made him the delight and terror of every conference he attended. I think all of us carry the scars, usually well deserved ones, which we received at Hedley's hands—all of us, that is, who were his contemporaries or seniors. Never did he inflict them on his pupils; and those who knew him only in later life when he became a magisterial, almost awe-inspiring figure, may find it hard to visualise what that earlier, ferocious *persona* had been like.

Hedley matured quickly when he returned to Australia to take up the Chair of International Relations at [The Australian National University in] Canberra.

I still saw him at conferences where he remained as refreshing and iconoclastic as ever. When to our delight he decided to apply for the Montague Burton Chair in Oxford, he named me as one of his referees, and among other things I wrote the following words:

> From his earliest days as a teacher it was clear that he brought to the study of International Relations a very remarkable mind: active, sceptical, analytic: the mind of a natural scientist or a philosopher rather than a historian. This approach was accompanied by a rather abrasive and arrogant manner which was, and is, not to everyone's taste, but which I believe masked, and still masks, the endearing uncertainties of a young man ill at ease in the salons of a richly corrupt Old World which he alternately admires and despises. Even now he cannot resist the occasional Antipodean temptation *epater le bourgeois*, especially if the bourgeois concerned is English and rather grand. His period as Director of the Arms Control and Disarmament Research Unit at the Foreign Office gave him plenty of opportunities for doing this, but the outstanding quality of his contributions to thinking about this fuzzy subject far outstripped any annoyance he may have caused. His little book *The Control of the Arms Race*, a classic of lucid judgement and common sense, had an international impact, on practitioners as well as theorists. It was a Cartesian contribution in that it was from that work (together with the contemporary American studies of, notably, Thomas Schelling) that all subsequent thinking about the place of armaments in international relations must be dated.

As a colleague I can say only that Hedley fulfilled, and more than fulfilled, all the hopes we had placed in him. But it was our common misfortune that within a very few years of his arrival here the economic Ice Age closed in, and so far from being able to expand its activities the university had to fight quite desperately to preserve those which were already in progress. There was no limit to the number of first-rate students Hedley could have attracted from all over the world: the bounds were set by the numbers of people available here to teach them. We were supremely fortunate in being able to raise the money to endow the Alastair Buchan Readership, and even luckier to get Adam Roberts to fill it. But without Hedley's reputation, drive, ingenuity and self-sacrifice (his teaching hours must have been astronomical) the whole enterprise would have withered, if not died. How far his incessant labours affected his health I cannot say, but certainly no consideration of his personal convenience, comfort, or even perhaps survival would have affected his determination to press on with them while there was still breath in his body.

By the end of his life, Hedley was well on the way to becoming one of those grand elder statesmen whom he used to tease when young. Election to the British

Academy came just in time for him to appreciate it. But in his case the grandeur came not from pomposity or self-importance but from a truly comprehensive vision of the world and a shrewd insight into affairs which gave his pronouncements an authoritative quality to which one listened with awe. His abrasiveness had softened into an ironical amusement, which in its silence could sometimes be more disconcerting than the direct assaults of his youth. He had achieved that most precious of all qualities, wisdom. But one still felt that there lurked, never far away, that impish desire to tease, if no longer to outrage, the bourgeois which kept him till the end of his life such a fundamentally youthful and such an endearing person; and which helps to explain why we miss him so much.

ENDNOTES

[1] This address was given as 'Hedley Bull: A Eulogy for his Memorial Service' at the memorial service to Hedley Bull on 17 October 1985. See Robert O'Neill and David N. Schwartz (eds), *Hedley Bull on Arms Control*, p. 276. The address is reprinted here with the kind permission of Professor Sir Michael Howard.

Appendix: The Hedley Bull Centre

The Hedley Bull Centre at The Australian National University was officially opened on 6 August 2008. Designed by award-winning Melbourne-based firm Lyons Architects, the Centre is located on the corner of Liversidge Street and Garran Road in the nation's capital, Canberra.

Adhering to the architectural firm's guiding philosophy 'form follows ideas', the Hedley Bull Centre is designed to enable and encourage dialogue between the staff and students of the various academic units who inhabit its corridors—interacting as parts of a whole for the common goals of rigorous academic scholarship and teaching excellence.

Focused on these goals, the Asia-Pacific College of Diplomacy, the Department of International Relations, the Department of Political and Social Change, and the Strategic and Defence Studies Centre moved into the Centre over one month prior to its official opening. This means that more than 120 individuals (including academic staff, visiting fellows, doctoral students and academic unit support staff) will work in the Centre. Each unit also has its own large library/reading room with windows that look out into a central atrium space, whilst a café will adjoin the Centre.

Large water retention tanks, a grey water system, double-glazing, high mass construction, and a 'mixed mode' climate control system have also been incorporated in the design and installed to ensure an environmentally sustainable Centre.

A variety of graduate programs within the academic units cater for numerous masters and graduate diploma students. For these students, and also for conferences and special events, the Hedley Bull Centre has modern, well-equipped facilities (including a seminar room, two lecture theatres and a computer lab).

Remembering Hedley describes Hedley Bull's life and work, including the time he spent at The Australian National University. The current Hedley Bull Fellow within the Centre is Mr Greg Fry in the Department of International Relations, and the Graduate Studies in International Affairs program offers up to four Hedley Bull Scholarships each year for full-time study in the Master of Arts (International Relations) program.

Many more individuals researching or teaching in the fields of diplomacy, international relations, political and social change, and strategy and defence will walk the Centre's corridors throughout the coming years.

And, finally, why Hedley Bull? The building serves as a fitting legacy to the extraordinary life and all-encompassing work of one of most formidable talents in the fields of international relations and strategic studies. As Bruce Miller notes in his chapter, 'we owe him so much'. The Australian National University 'is right to commemorate him with the opening of the Hedley Bull Centre'.

Appendix by Meredith Thatcher,
Strategic and Defence Studies Centre, July 2008

Main Entrance to the Hedley Bull Centre

Main Entrance to the Hedley Bull Centre

Main Entrance to the Hedley Bull Centre

Looking down on the atrium of the Hedley Bull Centre

View inside the APCD Lecture Theatre in the Hedley Bull Centre

Three levels of reading rooms in the Hedley Bull Centre

One of the reading rooms in the Hedley Bull Centre

View from a professorial office

Professorial office in the Hedley Bull Centre

View of Black Mountain and Telstra Tower from Level 4, Hedley Bull Centre

View of the corner of Liversidge Street and Garran Road (with parliament in the distance) from Level 4, Hedley Bull Centre

www.ingramcontent.com/pod-product-compliance
Lightning Source LLC
Chambersburg PA
CBHW061240270326

41927CB00035B/3460